Theology and Politics

Signposts in Theology

Theology, Death and Dying
Ray S. Anderson

Theology and Religious Pluralism
Gavin D'Costa

Theology and Philosophy
Ingolf U. Dalferth

Theology and Politics
Duncan B. Forrester

Theology and the Problem of Evil
Kenneth Surin

Theology and Literature
T. R. Wright

Other titles in preparation

Theology and Feminism
Daphne Hampson

Theology and Politics

DUNCAN B. FORRESTER

Basil Blackwell

First published 1988

Basil Blackwell Ltd
108 Cowley Road, Oxford, OX4 1JF, UK

Basil Blackwell Inc.
432 Park Avenue South, Suite 1503
New York, NY 10016, USA

British Library Cataloguing in Publication Data

Forrester, Duncan B.
  Theology and politics —— (Signposts in theology).
  1. Christianity and politics
  I. Title
  261.7   BR115.P7
  ISBN 0-631-15282-2
  ISBN 0-631-15283-0 Pbk

Library of Congress Cataloging in Publication Data

Forrester, Duncan.
  Theology and politics
  (Signposts in theology)
  Includes index
  1. Christianity and politics.   2. Liberation theology
  I. Title II. Series
  BR115.P7F67 1988   261.7   87-34109
  ISBN 0-631-15282-2
  ISBN 0-631-15283-0 (pbk.)

Typeset in 10 on 12 pt Century Oldstyle by Colset Private Ltd., Singapore
Printed in Great Britain by Billing & Sons Ltd, Worcester

Contents

For Donald and Catriona

Preface

This book aims to introduce political theology by exploring a few central themes and emphases in what is today a complex, controversial and fast-changing subject. It makes no claim to being a comprehensive text book or critical monograph. It is, according to the intention of the series, a signpost to a challenging field of action, reflection and debate, and an invitation to join in the 'doing' of political theology.

In a sense every religion and every political system must generate a political theology of some kind. Accordingly, in chapter 1 I survey the fascinating heritage of varying relationships between theology and politics to which early Christianity had to relate. I conclude by outlining the various types of political theology and approaches to understanding the relationship between Christian faith and the political realm which developed within the Christian tradition in the early centuries. These have continued as perennial options since then. This is not a history of political theology, but attention has had to be given to a few key moments in that history, and to some central themes which are of continuing relevance.

In a book such as this, it is necessary to be selective. I have chosen to give considerable attention to liberation theology in Latin America, with some mention also of debate in Korea, South Africa and elsewhere. This is, however, no arbitrary decision. Western Christians and theologians still have to face up to the challenge of this remarkable upsurge of action and reflection. It cannot be dismissed out of hand, and we need to expose ourselves to it with openness and sympathy before an adequate response or critical assessment will be possible. In chapter 7 and the second part of chapter 6 I make some tentative suggestions about how we might relate to this development, which is clearly of the greatest theological importance. Liberation theologians themselves remind us that it is not permissible for us to deck ourselves out in clothes we have borrowed from them. We have to allow liberation theology to provoke us to our own action and rigorous reflection in relation to our own Church and society, our own economic, political and cultural context, and our own responsibilities and opportunities.

Much remains to be done, and thought, and said. This book is intended to be an invitation to join in this venture. It is a signpost to a road that Western theology in recent years has been both reluctant and ill equipped to tread – seeking the Kingdom, with critical study and reflection ancillary to that goal.

My first debt in the preparation of this book must be to the students from various lands and backgrounds who have, over the past few years, discussed these themes in my political theology seminar. They have regularly stimulated, challenged and enlightened me. Several colleagues have commented helpfully on drafts; I am grateful in particular to Robin Gill and Ian McDonald for suggestions and for encouragement. Philip West has done me the considerable service of commenting in detail on two successive drafts. These friends have helped to improve the book, but should not be blamed for its inadequacies. My wife Margaret's love and support underlies this project, as all that I do, and her ministry provides a demonstration of the praxis of the Kingdom. Our children, Donald and Catriona, do not always agree with me by any means, but they care very passionately about the issues of justice, hope and human dignity with which political theology is concerned. I dedicate this book to them.

Some parts of chapter 7 have appeared in rather different form in my essay on 'The theological task' in Howard Davis (ed.) *Ethics and Defence* (Basil Blackwell, 1986) and in 'Mystique and politique' in Duncan Forrester and Alison Elliott (eds) *The Scottish Churches and the Political Process Today* (Edinburgh University Centre for Theology and Public Issues, 1986). The quotation on pages 73–4 from *Camilo Torres – Revolutionary Priest* is reproduced by kind permission of the editor, John Gerassi. Finally, I am grateful to my friend and former student, James Fields, for help with the proofs and for preparing the index.

Duncan B. Forrester

CHAPTER 1

Piety and Politics in the Ancient World

In a sense all societies have some kind of political theology, more or less developed, and articulated in a huge diversity of ways. But Christian political theology is in important ways distinctive, and reflects understandings of the nature, possibilities and limits of the political which are rooted deep in a Christian view of God and the world. The context out of which Christianity emerged illuminates the special characteristics and problems of Christian political theology and its relation to other approaches to understanding and assessing the political dimension of life. Accordingly, that context and some of the early history of Christian political theology will be examined in this chapter.

The kind of distinction between 'church' and 'state' to which we are so accustomed in the modern world is really rather unusual. In the ancient world, and in less complex societies today, it is difficult to distinguish clearly a religious from a political dimension of life, or to separate the believing community from the civil community. A people is defined in terms of the god worshipped. Each tribe, each caste, each village has its god or gods; to take part in the cult of these gods is a necessary sign of belonging; one cannot really be a member of the community without sharing in the worship of the community's gods. This is not a matter of free individual choice, but one of the fundamental obligations of community membership. For to worship the community's gods is to ensure the prosperity and security of the community, and to deny the gods worship is to threaten the life of the community itself – it is an attack on the community to which one belongs, and beyond that it is a threat to the cosmic order in which the human community has its place and on which it depends. The individual in such societies has no existence apart from the collective. Excommunication, exclusion from fellowship, is a kind of death, for the individual hardly exists apart from the community. The part depends upon the whole. The community is seen as a kind of organism; an amputated limb cannot survive on its own.

Through myths the individual learns his place in the community and the universe, and finds an explanation of his identity. In ancient societies two of the perennial functions of mythology were to elicit loyalty, and to show how the earthly political order was linked to the cosmic order. In mythology, temple, altar and deity not only correspond to palace, throne and king, but together they are the hub of the cosmic totality. Only in the frame of cosmology is it possible to understand politics, and both were interpreted in the light of myths. We should not therefore be surprised to find that a significant amount of myth is centrally concerned with political matters.

Each of the three main categories of myth identified by Henri Frankfort and his collaborators has a clear political reference. Myths of origin tell a story to explain how some part of reality came into being. Thus, in Rudyard Kipling's delightful series of invented myths, *The Just-So Stories*, a tale is told to explain how the elephant got his trunk. The myth or story does more than describe how something came into being; it also explains why it is like this and not otherwise; it provides a justification as well as a description. Myths of organization ask how some god or other being obtained particular functions or offices, how certain classes came to be higher in status than others and so on. And here, once more, the story that answers the question implies very strongly that these things *must be so*, that it is right and proper that they should be so. Myths of evaluation are really a sub-class of myths of organization. They affirm and give an odour of sanctity to the values implicit in the existing order. The king is majestic and must be obeyed because he participates in deity, or because he has the highest place in the earthly hierarchy which corresponds to the heavenly hierarchy (Frankfort et al., 1949, pp. 164–5).

Thus, for example, ancient Egyptian mythology depicted Pharaoh as himself one of the gods, the son of Re, the sun god. As such, he was a mediator between Egypt and the heavenlies, between the political and the cosmic. He represented the land and its people among the gods, and was on earth the personification of the power and graciousness of the gods. Egypt stood at the centre of the world, and the glory and power of the sun, the regularity of the Nile floods on which the crops depended, and the gracious rule of Pharaoh all spoke of a social and cosmic harmony which it would be catastrophic to disturb. The Mesopotamians, on the other hand, did not have the same assured sense of harmony. Order had to be struggled for, and earthly politics was seen as part of the cosmic struggle against chaos. The universe was ruled over by a council of gods who were by no means always in concord with one another. The human state was a kind of minor tributary of this cosmic state, ruled over by mortals appointed to this office by the divine council, who might have their authority withdrawn at any time, were not themselves divine, and did not participate in the divine council which appointed them (Frankfort et al., 1949; Morrison, 1960 pp. 70–2). Similar mythological systems could be instanced for most ancient societies of which we have knowledge.

Such ways of construing the world are, of course, highly conservative in their implications. To challenge the authorities is impious as well as seditious. Rebellion is an invitation to chaos – not simply in the sense of a breakdown of law and order, but as a fundamental disruption of the *cosmic* order, the regularity of the seasons, the fruitfulness of the soil and all that makes the world a place fit for humans to live in. Thus, political mythology provides more than explanations and justifications for the existing political order. It puts the ruler on a different plane from the people, subject to different rules and either responsible directly to the gods or himself divine. It insistently provides powerful supernatural sanctions to dissuade even the most foolhardy from tampering with the sacred political order or disturbing the cosmic equilibrium. Mythology thus qualifies as a potent method of social control.

It was much the same in the city-states of the ancient world. Here, piety and patriotism were virtually indistinguishable. The civic cult bound the citizens of the *polis* together in loyalty to one another and in service to the city's gods. Religion shaped the life of the city, gave it its laws and provided the sanctions for obedience. Each city had its god or gods who cared especially for it; there was little sense of universal deity. Conviction or doubt, emotion or detachment – all these were immaterial; the cult was a civil duty and no decent citizen would wish to disturb it.

Alongside the cult of the city's gods there flourished in increasing profusion as time went on a multitude of new sects and religions, mostly imported from the East. The ancient city was hospitable to any new faith as long as it did not make claims which conflicted directly with the civil religion, and was content to operate in a tolerant, syncretistic atmosphere. These new enthusiastic sects provided more emotionally charged forms of religion than the official cult and were a matter of individual choice. But within this syncretistic pluralism it was the cult of the gods of the city which legitimated the political order, and must be acknowledged at least formally by all citizens.

Civil religion in its classic form was found in the ancient Greek and Roman city-states. Here we can now clearly distinguish institutions in society which are recognized as 'religious', but these (or at least the most significant of them) are simply departments of state. Piety (the worship of the city's gods) and patriotism (loyalty to the city) are virtually one and the same. The city is watched over by its gods, who share in its joys and sorrows. Their cult is a celebration and an affirmation of the life of the city. Religion does not seek to change, challenge or question the established order; rather, it proclaims that it is god-given and sacrosanct. The ethics enjoined by the state and believed necessary for the state's prosperity is never in tension with a religious ethics. The pious person, the good person and the good citizen are all one. Adherence to religions of the heart or austere rationalist philosophies were both alike regarded as compatible with good citizenship *provided* that there was a formal ritual acknowledgement of the civil cult.

With the growth of the Roman empire came the development of a highly formal imperial cult which served the turn of a civil religion, eliciting and confirming loyalty to the empire but making few and infrequent demands, like Shintoism in modern Japan. Hospitality to a wide range of cults was seen as in no way incompatible with the maintenance of the civil cult, provided that these other religions made no universal or exclusive claims which conflicted with the special political position of the imperial cult and were willing either, like the mystery religions, to serve as voluntary embellishments to the official religion, or, like Judaism, were content to confine themselves, and their universalistic claims, to a social ghetto from which they posed no threat, protected by law as a *religio licita*. Those of a more rationalist cast of mind, who despised popular superstition, developed a philosophical monotheism which drew parallels between the one god in heaven and the one emperor on earth and provided a kind of theology for the imperial cult. This was not felt to be in any way incompatible with a civil religion intended primarily for the masses (Ehrhardt, 1959–69).

This mutually supportive relationship between religion and the political order did not go unquestioned. Four sorts of challenge deserve special consideration; the appeal to *nature*, the questioning of *critical philosophy*, the belief that the revealed *will of God* is superior to all human law, and the impact of *Christianity*.

NATURE

Tradition-directed societies (to use David Riesman's phrase) are in general content to understand the good in conventional terms (Riesman, 1951). It is what has always been done in our city; it is what our fathers did; it is elaborated and defended by reference to the city's gods. Our customs and traditions give us all the guidance that we need; our laws are absolutely binding. But this enclosed, tradition-bound mind-set was sharply disturbed by various factors which together forced the recognition of a diversity of morals and of gods. Different nations had different laws, sometimes in sharp conflict; not everyone agreed as to the good. Contacts with foreign countries revealed sharp differences of practice and belief. The Persian War of 521–479

B.C., together with increased trade around the Mediterranean basin and the establishment of colonies outside Greece, increased awareness of diversity. Herodotus, the historian of the Persian War, collected many accounts of varying customs and patterns of behaviour. He showed that this new knowledge made it impossible to accept in the traditional unquestioning way the laws and customs of one's own community.

If *nomos* (law or custom) is recognized as varying from one society to another, there are three possibilities open. One may reaffirm the absolute validity of one's own tradition, customs, laws, and dismiss all other ways of life as deviant, comic or childish. Such defensive reactions have been common from the days of the Greek city-states in the sixth century B.C. to the present day. A second response is a rather cynical relativism; awareness of diversity of morals shows that there is no such thing as the good, or the true or the beautiful; no criterion against which the *nomos* of a society may be judged. This was the line generally adopted by the Sophists, who were accused by Socrates of manipulating the situation to their personal advantage. Recognizing no universal moral principles applying to human beings as such, and with their loyalty to the laws and customs of their own city undercut by the awareness of the diversity of morals, they set out to pursue their own interests, particularly in securing power for themselves.

Others sought out a principle which was universal, which applied everywhere and always and to everyone, against which the standards of societies and individuals might be measured. This must be something which applies to people as people, not as citizens of some particular state or society, something to which Greeks, Persians and Egyptians may equally appeal. In nature (*phusis*) it was felt that the clue was to be found. The great processes of nature – growth and decay, the rising and setting of the sun, the rotating seasons, and so forth – were to be found everywhere; nature always followed the same 'laws' or rules. If analogous moral and political principles could be found, we would indeed have the universal and unchanging guidance which was desired. And nature was understood as charged with purpose, and as an expression of the unchanging will of God. So we find already in ancient Greek philosophy the beginnings of a theory of natural law, essentially the same but operating in two related realms – the natural and the moral order, both understood in teleological terms, as hastening towards their goal. Natural law then stands over the law of the particular state; it is a standard against which the laws and customs of each society may be judged. The legislator should seek to express the natural law in the laws of the state, and the citizen may appeal from the judgements of the ruler to a higher standard, that of natural law.

In Sophocles' (*c.*496–406 B.C.) great tragedy, *Antigone*, the king of Thebes, Creon, decrees in accordance with the customs (*nomos*) of the city that the body of Polynices, who died attacking the city, should be left to rot, unburied and without the usual obsequies, while his brother, Eteocles, who died defending the city, receives an honourable burial. Creon's edict is based on his care for the welfare of the city:

> Our country is our life; only when she
> Rides safely, have we any friends at all,
> Such is my policy for our common weal . . .
> I am determined that never, if I can help it,
> Shall evil triumph over good. Alive
> Or dead, the faithful servant of his country
> Shall be rewarded.
>
> (Sophocles, 1947 edn, pp. 131–2)

The edict is defended, as many political acts are today, by reference to the national interest and the customs of the people.

But Antigone, sister of Polynices and Eteocles, disobeys the order and herself give Polynices a ceremonial burial. She is arrested, and defends her act by appealing to a higher court and a higher law, a law which is universal, the law of nature and of nature's God, not just the god of Thebes. Antigone stands before Creon:

> That order did not come from God, Justice,
> That dwells with the gods below, knows no such law.
> I do not think your edicts strong enough
> To overrule the unwritten unalterable laws
> Of God and heaven, you being only a man.

They are not of yesterday or to-day, but everlasting,
Though where they come from none of us can tell.
Guilty of their transgression before God
I cannot be, for any man on earth.

(Sophocles, 1947 edn, p. 138)

Nature, nature's God and natures' law – on this foundation was erected a great tradition of philosophical and theological reflection on politics.

CRITICAL PHILOSOPHY

Socrates may stand as the epitome of the critical philosopher whose relentless questioning is profoundly corrosive of the traditional political theology and civil religion. Unlike the Sophists, he asserted the possibility of knowledge of the good. The philosophic life was a search for this knowledge. It involved a style of living appropriate to this search, not just a way of thinking. It led him to ruthless interrogation of all who had any pretensions to knowledge, and his questioning of the politicians made it obvious to everyone that they did not know what they were doing, and were operating with radically inadequate principles. He saw his vocation as that of a kind of irritant, 'a sort of gadfly, given to the state by God': 'I am that gadfly which God has attached to the state, and all day long and in all places I am always fastening upon you, arousing and persuading and reproaching you' (Jowett, 1945, p. 76).

Socrates himself worshipped the gods of the city, was a scrupulously loyal citizen and boasted of his patriotism, but he was condemned for misleading the youth and teaching atheism. 'Socrates is a doer of evil, who corrupts the youth', his accusers said: 'and he does not believe in the gods of the state but has other new divinities of his own' (Jowett, 1945, p. 65). And in a sense he was indeed one who undercut the old civil religion and political theology in an irreversible way. His disciples were taught to question and to think for themselves, and thus emancipated themselves from the old solidarities and the inherited reverence for tradition which were integral to civil religion. 'Men of Athens,' Socrates affirmed at his trial, 'I honour and love you; but I shall obey God rather than you, and while I have life and strength I shall never cease from the practice and teaching of philosophy' (Jowett, 1945, p. 74). By asserting the right to doubt and to question, he implied in no uncertain fashion that the *polis* was not holy and beyond scrutiny. As Fustel de Coulanges argues, he 'founded a new religion, which was the opposite of the city religion. He was justly accused of not adoring the gods whom the state adored' (de Coulanges, 1956, p. 356).

Despite itself, as it were, the impact of critical philosophy was destructive of the traditional civil religion and the inherited political theology. But there was also a positive side. The city had been a self-contained sacral universe with hardly any interest in the destiny of the individual or in responsibilities to humankind. Philosophy now taught the individual that he was more than a citizen, a creature of the community. The individual was enjoined to 'Know thyself', and to be obedient above all to the voice of conscience; a tension was recognized as emerging between what it means to be a good man and a good citizen; and the immortality of the good man's soul was stressed – even if that good man, like Socrates, was condemned to death by the city for breach of its law and conventions. Neither goodness nor truth, Socrates suggests, can be defined or controlled by the state, and the one who is committed to the search for these universal values which transcend the realm of politics passes at death into an immortality where the *polis* cannot touch him. Already there are clear hints of a new and quite different political theology and political philosophy struggling to be born, not circumscribed by the limits of the state but dealing with the relation between the civil community and that which transcends, challenges and gives meaning to the political.

THE REVEALED WILL OF GOD

Judaism, as found in the Roman empire, did not fit neatly into the generally accepted pattern of a 'religion'. In the Diaspora it differed from the profusion of religions and cults, old and new, which were tolerated and indeed encouraged alongside the civil cult in that it resisted strenuously and successfully being enrolled into the syncretistic amalgam which was the cultic legitimation of the Roman empire. But, confined to the ghetto, it could hardly corrupt the multifaceted civil religion of the empire by spreading, save in very limited intellectual circles. In some significant respects, however, Judaism was similar to the other major religions of the ancient world. Neither in the ghetto nor in Israel was there a clear distinction between the religious community and the political community; faith was understood as shaping the life of the whole community; citizenship of Israel was seen as inseparable from the faith of Israel; and the Torah which shaped the common life was understood as the revealed will of God.

The universalistic strain in the Old Testament became increasingly dominant in the Diaspora communities. The God of Israel is the God of all, the universal Lord, who is most clearly acknowledged and understood in Israel. Yahweh stands over his people in promise and judgement. Rulers, even Gentile emperors, may be in some sense agents of Yahweh, but they do not participate in divinity. This was held despite the fact that sometimes in the Old Testament, particularly in the Psalms, divine honours and titles are indeed accorded to earthly rulers. The political power God entrusts to men and women is always conditional; no one is unqualifiedly the representative of God. Rulers stand under God's will and God's law and are always answerable to God, who is a God of justice, not of arbitrary power, a God who has a special care for the poor and the weak.

This prophetic and deuteronomic strand in the Old Testament sees the social and political order as created by God. But it does not from that fact derive any inherent sanctity. It stands under the judgement and promise of God. It is not holy and beyond question. Indeed, there is a recognition that all earthly structures tend to diverge from the will of the God of justice. God is often celebrated as the one who *reverses* the existing order, as in Hannah's prayer (I Sam. 2: 1–10) with which the Magnificat may be compared (Luke 1: 46–55):

There is none holy like the Lord,
there is none besides thee;
there is no rock like our God . . .
The bows of the mighty are broken,
but the feet of the feeble gird on strength.
Those who were full have hired themselves out for bread,
but those who were hungry have ceased to hunger . . .
He raises up the poor from the dust;
he lifts the needy from the ash heap,
to make them sit with princes and inherit a seat of honour.
For the pillars of the earth are the Lord's
and on them he has set the world.

(I Sam. 2: 2–8)

The contrast between this sort of attitude and the tendency of most ancient cultures to regard the social and political orders as sacred, and any threat to them as impious and an invitation to chaos is marked. The polity and the social order are neither sacred nor autonomous; God's will is to be done here at least as much as in the personal life of the individual. Yahweh transcends all earthly things, but he gathers a people to himself to live according to his will and show his justice as a 'light to lighten the gentiles'.

EARLY CHRISTIANITY

Jesus the Jew came to proclaim the good news of the Kingdom of God; 'The time is fulfilled, and the Kingdom of God is at hand; repent, and believe in the gospel' (Mark 1: 15). The Kingdom – or, more accurately, the 'kingly rule of God' – is the principal theme of the teaching of Jesus, providing a framework for understanding the significance of the person and the work of Jesus and indeed suggesting a whole interpretation of history. The nature of the Kingdom of God is shown in the activity and the teaching of Jesus of Nazareth. His healings, his feeding of the hungry crowds, his care for folk in need are all seen as signs of the Kingdom. When John the Baptist is arrested by Herod and, languishing in prison, begins to doubt whether Jesus is in fact the promised one who is to come, he sends his disciples to enquire of Jesus: 'Are you he who is to come, or shall we look for another?' (Luke 7: 20). Jesus's response is to tell them to report to John what they have heard and seen, for these are the signs of the Kingdom, the proof that the Messianic age is dawning. The miracles attest that the powers of evil are being put to flight, that God's just and compassionate ordering of things is being restored in and through Jesus. And the teaching of Jesus, particularly the parables of the Kingdom, points to the initiative that is being taken by God, creating a crisis in which a prompt and costly and unconditional response is called for. The Kingdom has been inaugurated by Jesus, but its final culmination is still to come. Hence the disciples are taught to pray 'Your Kingdom come', and wait the final consummation of God's purposes which have been definitively manifested in Jesus.

For our present purposes the most important thing to notice is that the new age is presented in political terms. The goal is not, as in much eastern religion, the reabsorption of the individual into the All, so that earthly particularities are overcome and 'the drop returns to the ocean of Being', nor is it the direct fellowship between the believer and the Lord in which all others are forgotten which some pietists seem to expect. Rather surprisingly, it is not the glorification of the Church, and the gathering of all into the fellowship of believers to participate in the heavenly worship of God. Indeed, the opposite seems to be the case, as the imaginative portrayal of the New Jerusalem in Revelation 21 suggests, for in that city there is no temple; it remains a politically structured community but has no need of cult, temple or religion. These things have passed away with the new age – but not the Kingdom, or the City in which God reigns, and into which he gathers his people. These central images in the New Testament – the Kingdom of God, the City and the New Jerusalem – suggest an order that Jesus has inaugurated and outlined, into which people are called, but which is not yet present in its fullness. Because their true citizenship is there, not here, Christians know that they have 'no continuing city' on earth (Heb. 13: 14); Christians are exiles and sojourners because their citizenship is in heaven. And that citizenship and that Kingdom have a profound bearing on earthly citizenship and the life of earthly cities and kingdoms. As Karl Barth put it: 'In this future city in which Christians have their citizenship here and now (without yet being able to inhabit it), we are concerned not with an ideal but with a real State – yes, with the only real State; not with an imaginary one but with the only one that truly exists' (Barth, 1939, p. 38).

As in the Old Testament, it is affirmed that the true King of Israel is Yahweh, whoever may actually be ruling on earth, so now the universalistic strands in the Old Testament are developed further to affirm the universal, all-encompassing sovereignty of God in the Kingdom inaugurated by Jesus. This Kingdom is open to all; it is not an ethnic reserve. All nations and cultures are welcome in the Kingdom and in the New Jerusalem, which comes down 'out of heaven from God, prepared as a bride adorned for her husband' (Rev. 21: 2). In this inclusivism Christianity diverged momentously from the almost universal assumption of ancient religions that each god protected only the family, the tribe, the city or the empire that owed the god allegiance. Entry to the Kingdom may be offered first to the Jews, but it is in principle open to all. Citizenship of the Kingdom is thus in tension with narrower loyalties, including earthly citizenship. The old suspicions and hostilities between those of different communities, cultures and societies are overcome by Christ who 'has broken down the dividing wall of hostility', the paradigmatic gulf between Jews and Gentiles, in order to make peace; and now Jew and Gentile are 'no longer strangers and sojourners, but fellow citizens with the saints and members of the household of God (Eph. 2: 14–19). 'For this God, as Fustel de Coulanges says, 'there were no longer strangers' (de Coulanges, 1956, p. 392).

Furthermore, the reality and power of the civil gods of the ancient world have necessarily to be denied as incompatible with the claims of the God and Father of Jesus Christ. Refusal of worship to the countless gods and goddesses of the ancient world did not, of course, involve denying to earthly rulers, who saw themselves as divine or as agents of the gods, obedience, respect, honour and prayers. But the denial of their legitimating theology and divine pretensions served in an important way to secularize politics – to cut it down to size. And, simultaneously, it affirmed that the civil power could not expect of its citizens the kind of uncritical, absolute loyalty that was usually expected. The individual is more than the creature of the state, there are limits to the state's claims upon its citizens, and human destiny points beyond the state. In a sense the state was set free from religious control, and simultaneously it was cut down to size and deprived of its religious pretensions. As Fustel de Coulanges puts it:

> On the one hand, politics became definitively freed from the strict rules which the ancient religion had traced, and could govern men without having to bend to sacred usages, without consulting the auspices or the oracles, without conforming all acts to the beliefs and requirements of a worship. Political action was freer; no other authority than that of the moral law now impeded it. On the other hand, if the state was more completely master in certain things, its action was also more limited. A complete half of man had been freed from its control. Christianity taught that only a part of man belonged to society.
>
> (de Coulanges, 1956, p. 395)

The change was massive, but the break from the past was far from total. Albeit in radically different fashion, politics, the state and political activity were still seen as intimately related to God's purposes and as requiring theological interpretation. Early Christianity undertook this interpretation, using its own distinctive materials for the reconstruction of political theology.

MATERIALS FOR CHRISTIAN POLITICAL THEOLOGY

'Jesus is Lord (*kurios*)' was probably the earliest confessional formula of the Christian Church, used in all probability at baptisms (Rom.10: 9; Phil.2: 11). The Greek word *kurios* was used in the Greek version of the Old Testament as the name of God, and it was commonly applied also to earthly rulers. In Acts 25: 26, for instance, the Roman governor, Festus, refers to the Emperor as Lord (*kurios*). The primitive confession is therefore clearly affirming the divine status of Jesus, and also claiming for him a title commonly assumed by emperors and rulers. *Kurios*, in short, connotes an office which is both spiritual and political. The same is true of the term Anointed One, *messiah* in Hebrew and *christ* in Greek. The Messiah is the one who is to come to inaugurate the kingly rule of God and restore Israel. The Messiah was generally expected to come as a king who would deliver his people and rule them in righteousness, the 'Son of David' whom God would send to restore the Davidic kingdom among his people.

Jesus, according to the synoptic gospel accounts, never called himself the Messiah, and when Peter confessed him to be the Christ, Jesus binds the disciples to secrecy (Mark 8: 29–30; cf Luke 9: 20–1; Matt.16: 13–20). In John's gospel, on the other hand, Jesus quite openly asserts that he is the Messiah (John 4: 25–6; 10: 24–5). But in all the gospels, Jesus is sent to death as the King of the Jews, as a pretended Messiah. We do not need here to pursue the complex questions of whether Jesus in fact claimed to be the Messiah or was aware of being the Messiah, or the interpretation of the passages in the synoptics which deal with the 'Messianic secret'. What is important for us is that the early Christian belief that Jesus was the Christ carried with it expectations of a purely political deliverance and an exclusively Jewish salvation which had to be repudiated if a proper understanding of, and response to, Jesus were to be possible. Even those closest to him could not understand how the Messiah could suffer, and they continued after the resurrection to look to Jesus for the fulfilment of the nationalistic hope of the restoration of the kingdom of Israel (Acts 1: 6–8). Both *kurios* and *messiah*, then, were political titles claimed for Jesus and applied to him, but with their meaning radically changed to accommodate the new usage, yet without losing a political reference.

What is the relation of the lordship of Jesus Christ and the mysterious 'principalities and powers' which appear so frequently in the New Testament epistles, along with thrones, rulers, angels and so forth? Who, or what, are the 'rulers of this age' who are 'doomed to pass away', who do not understand the purposes of God, who 'have crucified the king of glory' (I Cor.2: 6–8)? Are we to think of these angelic powers as some kind of continuation of the old style of mythical thinking about politics, a way of relating the political and the cosmic orders? It is certainly interesting and intriguing that all these terms may be used quite directly of political rulers or of spiritual powers – or perhaps of both? Certainly they seem to suggest a mythical world view very alien to ours, populated with good and evil spirits. Thus the writer of Ephesians tells the readers that, 'We are not contending against flesh and blood, but against the principalities, against the powers, against the world rulers of this present darkness, against the spiritual hosts of wickedness in the heavenly places' (Eph. 6: 12), while in Colossians worship of angels is characteristic of those who have not yet died with Christ to the elemental spirits of the universe and still live in a worldly way (Col. 2: 20). And in other places – most notably Romans 13 – believers are enjoined to be subject to the 'powers' since they have been instituted and given their authority by God, and are God's servants. In Christ God 'disarmed the principalities and powers and made a public example of them, triumphing over them in him [Christ]' (Col. 2: 15); the spirits which were enemies are restored to their proper role, their demonic pretensions restrained, and they become 'ministering spirits sent forth to serve' (Heb. 1: 14). The implication of this language, that state and political activity have profound spiritual significance, is important in any context (Barth, 1939, pp. 23–36; Cullmann, 1951, 1957; Morrison, 1960; Wink, 1984).

While it may well be impossible to produce a fully coherent interpretation of the New Testament references to 'principalities and powers', two points deserve to be noted. First, this language provided the early Church with a way of interpreting and responding to the fact that earthly authority, established by God for the good of human beings, can and does from time to time degenerate, reject its divine mandate and act in a demonic manner. In other words, the believer is called to assesss the powers in the light of what is known of God's purposes and God's kingdom and adapt behaviour to this assessment. In contrast to most political mythologies, the powers are no longer seen as having an inherent holiness, however they behave; these de-sacralized powers may become radically evil by rebelling against the God who established them to do his will. But even such demonic powers cannot finally or effectively overturn the purposes of God shown in Jesus Christ; their rebellion is doomed to furstration because the ultimate victory has already been won, and all that remains is 'mopping-up operations' and sporadic, fierce but unsuccessful counter-attacks. Thus, even in dealing with obscene tyrannies like Nazism, Christians like Barth could see in the state a divine order which has been perverted and needs to be restored, and are sustained by a hope springing from their knowledge of the overarching sovereignty of God. Secondly, the principalities and powers have been disarmed, defeated, restored to their proper subordination to God. The significance of this vivid poetic language must surely by in part that Christians have been emancipated from the service of the powers, that they have entered into the glorious liberty of the children of God and are no longer enthralled by thrones, dominions and powers. They may now deal with the political realm as it really is; politics has been demystified; it is no longer an enchanted area, but it has profound spiritual significance. With the subduing of the powers, the old political religion and the old political theology have been fundamentally undercut.

We have seen how in the Old Testament there developed a distinctive conviction that Yahweh stands over both ruler and people in promise and judgement; he cannot be identified with either. Out of this there emerges a distinction between a political ethic and a religious ethic in as far as the will of the king or the canons of political prudence or expediency cannot be simply labelled the will of God. This distinction between two realms and two ethics is integral to the New Testament. For various reasons – particularly the expectation of the imminence of the end, and the fact that the early Church was a small minority sect – the New Testament does not contain more than fragments and hints of a political ethic, either understood as guidance for rulers and those in authority or as a normative model along the lines of the Old Testament law books of how a society under God should be organized. There are, to be sure, substantial treatments of individual and family ethics, and the norms of behaviour which are expected to be observed within the Christian fellowship. But when Christians have sought the principles by which a society should be framed in a Christian way, they have had recourse primarily to the Old Testament for guidance.

In the New Testament, however, there are clear attempts to relate God's sovereignty to earthly political power (Rowland, 1985; Sanders, 1985). The nature of the relationship is highlighted in John's account of the confrontation between Pilate and the bound, powerless Jesus, already condemned by the religious authorities. Jesus is in Pilate's power, as Pilate reminds him: 'Do you not know that I have power to release you, and power to crucify you?' (John 19: 10). Jesus replies that this power of Pilate's is 'from above', that it comes from God, that Pilate is responsible to God. And even Pilate, the tyrant who for reasons of timidity and expediency is to deliver Jesus to his death, is constrained to recognize the innocence of Jesus: 'I find no crime in him' (John 19: 4). All four gospels affirm that Pilate found Jesus innocent, 'a just man', and thus fulfilled one of the proper tasks of a ruler (Matt. 27: 19–24; Mark 15: 14; Luke 23: 14–15, 22; John 18: 38; 19: 4, 6). But through cowardice he did not take the logical next step – acquittal – but delivered Jesus to his death, thus denying the mandate given to him by God, abusing the power entrusted to him – as has happened again and again throughout history. Note, finally, that Pilate, with Jesus in his power, is implicated in the drama of redemption. He does not act in a different arena, another world, but the same world, the same community in which salvation is achieved. And his political activity becomes part of the drama of salvation. The whole passion narrative from the cleansing of the temple to the execution itself is particularly rich in themes which stimulate political theological reflection.

THE EMERGENCE OF CHRISTIAN POLITICAL THEOLOGY

It was inevitable that the early Christians, standing as they did in the Jewish tradition, should reject the civil religion and the political theology of the Roman world. At its simplest, they believed that loyalty to Jesus Christ was incompatible with participation in the rituals of the imperial cult, and that theology was concerned with the interpretation of life in the light of God's purposes, not the legitimation and sanctification of any political order. Although the New Testment suggests that the early Christians were capable of denouncing an emperor as the Beast of Revelation 13, on the whole they respected and obeyed the emperor and other political authorities, and they prayed for them to God, but they could not and would not accord them divine honours. Accordingly, they were accused of being atheists (like Socrates, centuries before in Athens), suspected of disloyalty and periodically subjected to violent persecution. Some of them, like Justin Martyr, were happy to call themselves atheists; loyal to the empire they might claim to be, but they would have nothing to do with the gods of the empire, and this kind of atheism was in the eyes of many inherently seditious.

But Christianity could not survive, spread and grow in size and influence, without generating a political theology, or rather a variety of political theologies, of its own. There were, of course, distinctive problems in this development. Was it possible to construct a political theology which had at its heart Jesus Christ, the suffering, humiliated one, condemned by the political authorities and the religious leadership and deserted by the people, whose throne paradoxically was a cross? It was easier to see Jesus as the *end* of all political theology than as the source of new, and different, political theology. Again, a strict philosophical monotheism might have provided a basis for a political theology which gave an interpretation and justification of the centralized authority of the Roman empire and its universalistic claims, but Christianity was a *trinitarian* faith, rejecting both the polytheism of the ancient world and a rigid philosophical monotheism in favour of an understanding of God as more like a community than an individual or a monad (Peterson, 1935; Moltmann, 1947b, 1975, 1981).

We shall suggest later that Christianity brought to the ancient world new and refreshing notions of community rooted in the doctrine of the trinity. But the same doctrine was deeply corrosive of the most obvious kind of theological legitimation of the empire, and of the religion that sustained the political order. The temptation was to suggest a simple and mutually supportive analogy between the one Church and the one empire, between the one God and the one emperor, between the *Pax Romana* and the Peace of God. But this was only possible by forgetting the suffering Jesus, the trinitarian nature of Christian faith and the eschatological expectation which declares the provisionality of even the best of earthly orderings. On such grounds Erik Peterson (1935) could argue that no Christian political theology is possible. But political theology as a theological interpretation of what is happening in the realm of politics and an attempt to relate to the varied forms of political religion which emerge in every age is inevitable, and has been there from the beginning, in diverse forms (Moltmann, 1975, pp. 101–18; 1981, pp. 190–202).

The range of attempts at the development of a Christian political theology which emerged in the early centuries following the death of Christ form a kind of spectrum. At one extreme are positions which we shall link with the name of Tertullian. At the other end lies the court theology of the empire developed by Eusebius. Augustine's prodigious achievement is somewhere in the middle. This spectrum also outlines the perennial possibilities for Christian political theology.

For Tertullian (*c.*160–220) the Church was a kind of counter-culture, and Christians were called to separate themselves from the *massa perditionis* which was secular society, rushing to its doom. 'There is nothing more alien to us than politics', he pronounced (*Apologeticus* 38: 3), and went on to argue that 'the fact that Christ rejected an earthly kingdom should be enough to convince you that all secular powers and dignities are not merely alien from but hostile to, God.' Christians belong to a 'counter-kingdom' in which:

> We are a body knit together as such by a common religious profession, by unity of discipline, and by the bond of a common hope ... Your citizenship, your magistracies, and the very name of your curia is the Church of Christ ... You are an alien in this world, and a citizen of the city of Jerusalem that is above.
>
> (*Apologeticus* 39; *De Corona* 13)

'Nothing', he writes, 'is more foreign to us than the state. One state we know, of which all are citizens – the universe' (*Apologeticus* 38). Within the Church, Christians live by their own standards, maintaining an absolutist ethic with a tendency to pacifism and a millenarian expectation that the end for the delaying of which they pray (*Apologeticus* 31) is at hand. This pure Church is to have no responsibility for power or any involvement in the world of politics. The Church is a parallel community which represents a challenge to political society because it stands for an alternative way of ordering life. But the challenge is indirect. As the *Epistle to Diognetus* (Apostolic Fathers, 1867 edn), a second- or third-century document which appears to come from this kind of circle, suggests, Christians are law-abiding citizens, who perform all their civic duties save for participating in the civic cult, follow a rigorist ethic and in fact sustain the civil community by their prayers, although they will not defend it by violence or take part in ruling. Sheldon Wolin (1961, pp. 96–7) argues that it was precisely this withdrawal from politics in order to sustain a fellowship of love without compromises with power which enabled Christianity to revitalize political thought. This alternative society or counter-kingdom understood itself as the soul giving life to the body politic, but it was also a challenge to the state and 'a new and sorely needed source of ideas for Western political thought'. That such a sectarian approach could produce an influential political theology should serve as a reminder of the value of concentration on the Gospel and the inner life of the Church. These matters may seem at times not to be directly relevant or applicable in the political realm. But this does not mean that they do not at a deeper level have a significant and distinctive contribution to make to political understanding and political action.

At the other end of the spectrum we place Eusebius of Caesarea (264–340), who sought to provide a political theology in the classical mode suitable for the new relationship between Church and empire which followed the Constantinian settlement, the recognition of Christianity as the established and official faith. Christianity was already taking over the traditional role of a civil religion, sacralizing power, legitimating the existing order of things and inculcating in the populace reverence for the authorities and obedience to orders. Eusebius now provided the theory to undergird this praxis, and to christianize popular attitudes towards the empire. In God's providence, Christianity and the Roman empire, the two greatest blessings to humankind, had arisen virtually simultaneously and now flowed together in the Christian emperor, Constantine:

> By the express appointment of the same God, two roots of blessing, the Roman Empire and the doctrine of Christian piety, sprang up together for the benefit of men .... [With the reign of Constantine] a new and fresh era of existence had begun to appear, and a light hitherto unknown suddenly dawned from the midst of darkness on the human race: and all must confess that these things were entirely the work of God, who raised up this pious emperor to withstand the multitude of the ungodly.
>
> *(Vita Constantini* II, 1; quoted in Wolin, 1961, p. 121)

Together, Church and empire may establish a lasting peace and justice in the world, which is more than a foreshadowing of the coming Kingdom; indeed, in the theology of Eusebius eschatological hopes are almost submerged beneath the glory of present reality. Church and state are in such perfect harmony that it poses no threat for the Church to become a department of the empire – Eusebius translates the pagan cult of the emperor into Christian terms and in the process Christianity came increasingly to mirror significant features and fulfil major functions of the old paganism.

Eusebius' theology is more monotheistic than trinitarian. The one God in heaven is reflected in the one emperor on earth; monotheism supports monarchy. But, as a Christian, he must admit that Christ, the *logos*, is also divine and deserving of worship. He ends up as a rather disjointed binitarian, clearly influenced by Arianism. Constantine emerges as a kind of Messianic figure; the banquets he gives to his bishops are like the Messianic feast; he is almost a fresh manifestation of the *logos*, another Christ (Young, 1983, pp. 1–22). It is not surprising that it has been argued that this establishment of the Christian faith was simultaneously its subversion (Kee, 1982). Christianity did not fit easily into the pagan mould of a civil religion, and Christian theology was radically distorted by becoming this kind of political theology. But the fact that Eusebius and his followers were much too ready to compromise, accommodate and acquiesce should not blind us to the need in every age for serious attempts to relate the Christian faith to new and unprecedented responsibilities.

Eusebius is the apologist for imperial rule and the propagator of a Christian civil religion; he sees the earthly role of the emperor as a reflection of, and a kind of participation in, the kingly omnipotence of God himself. The emperor is God's vice-regent and representative on earth. Hence, opposition to the emperor is opposition to the God he represents, and sedition and heresy are seen as closely linked, as are piety and patriotism. The state is sacralized once more. This is political theology in the classical tradition, continuous in style, function and, to some extent, content with the political theologies of the pagan emperors.

Somewhere around the centre of the spectrum of possible Christian political theologies we must place the towering figure of St Augustine (353–430). His great work, *De civitate Dei*, was occasioned by the suggestion that the sack of Rome by Alaric the Goth in 410 had been caused by the abandonment of the old civil religion of Rome: the gods of Rome were angry and the virtues that had been nurtured by the traditional patriotic cult were no more in evidence. Theologians of the school of Eusebius were incapable of responding to this onslaught because for them the prosperity and power of Rome were attributed to the favour of God, and there was no place in their understanding of providence for any reverse to Roman power; they could not accommodate within their theology of history the decline and fall of the Roman empire because in their thinking that empire and the Kingdom of God had become hopelessly confused. Augustine produced not simply a tract for the times, but a theology of history and a political theology which was one of the greatest achievements of late antiquity and a classic of Christian thought. *The City of God* was both 'a deliberate confrontation with paganism' (Brown, 1967, p. 312) and a major constructive endeavour which has had an immense impact on Western thought.

In sharp contrast to Eusebius, Augustine taught that the Roman empire was, and always had been, corrupt. Romulus, who murdered his brother, founded Rome with a gang of robbers. This is portrayed as typical of the earthly city: states, without justice are but bands of robbers, and robber bands are states in miniature (*De civitate Dei* III: 4). Notice here the emphasis on the importance of justice. Without it, a state becomes demonic; but it is also possible for a state in its ordering and its activity to manifest much, but not all of the justice which is necessary for human dignity and the flourishing of society. And 'justice' is redefined by Augustine. It is not understood primarily in legal or philosophical terms, but rather as something to be measured against the divine justice and love which is revealed in Jesus Christ and fully realized only in the City of God. Thus the earthly city, the *civitas terrena*, is fragmented, partial, incomplete, aiming at a provisional and always tenuous peace and justice arising out of the balancing of claims and interests. This relative peace and justice is a good necessary for stable social life, but it is not the highest good, which can only be found in the constant felicity of the City of God. No one should owe an absolute allegian ce to the earthly city; human beings seek a higher good than that of the earthly city, their true citizenship is elsewhere and they owe total allegiance only to God and his City.

The *civitas Dei*, by contrast, transcends the earthly city, but is relevant to both understanding and behaviour in the earthly city. The City of God is in principle a universal society overcoming all limited associations of state, class or race. One enters by grace – the Fall implies that the city of God is not a natural community to which all belong by virtue of nature; it is a God-centred fellowship, the members of which 'enjoy community with God and with one another in God'. Augustine defines a commonwealth as, 'A gathering of a multitude of rational beings united in fellowship by sharing a common love of the same things' (*De civitate Dei* XIX: 24). There are, of course, many loves which may bind people together in fellowship, but the highest love, which is the love of God, is the love which sustains the City of God, where alone true justice, true peace and true fellowship are to be found.

The Church as it exists on earth is a 'mixed body' of the elect and also of others and cannot simply be identified with the City of God. In this, Augustine differs from the tendency of such as Tertullian to absolutize the ecclesiastical institution, understood in a rather sectarian (and unrealistic?) way as a 'pure church'. Augustine sees the Church as a sign and partial manifestation of the City of God, so that he can say: 'The Church now on earth is both the Kingdom of Christ and the kingdom of heaven. The saints reign with him now, but not as they shall do hereafter' (*De civitate Dei* XX: 9). The City of God is an eschatological or heavenly reality, and the so-called 'political Augustinianism', which in the Middle Ages used Augustine's name to support the claims of the Church and the papacy to a kind of universal political sovereignty, was a gross distortion of the subtle thinking of St Augustine. For Augustine did not believe in the politicization of the Church, although he was convinced that the existence on earth of the church as a witness to the City of God and an expression of the love of God in contrast to the lust for glory and power in the *civitas terrena* was of immense importance for the life of the polity, in setting goals, in denouncing the abuse of power and in offering guidance. He was convinced that the Church on earth had a responsibility to defend peace and justice. This made the Church a consciously political body, capable of sustaining a new tradition of civility through the barbarian invasions and the Dark Ages (Ehrhardt, 1969, p. 51).

Augustine has a *political* theology, it is true, sparking between the two poles of the *civitas terrena* and the *civitas Dei*, but he holds back resolutely from deifying any temporal order or earthly ruler – or even the Church as an institution in this age, for that matter – as he strives to discern the signs of the times, the clues to God's working in history. Indeed, he boldly renders the pretensions of earthly power relative. Like Eusebius, he affirms the theological significance of the political order but, unlike Eusebius, he refuses to accord more than a heavily qualified endorsement to any temporal political order whatever. Secular politics is taken seriously by Augustine, but relentlessly excluded from the sphere of the sacred. He refuses to assimilate the two cities to one another, and judges that even a

Christian civil government is no more than a temporary and relative expedient. Politics requires to be nourished and challenged by the gospel; only in its relation to the City of God is it possible to understand the earthly city aright as either a band of robbers being drawn by their lust for power and riches towards perdition, or a fellowship of pilgrims lovingly seeking the City whose builder and maker is God.

CHAPTER 2

The Private and the Political

Alongside the demanding formal and public political religions of the Graeco-Roman world, there existed a multitude of cults, devotions and sects which could be freely chosen by the individual and which related to the heart and personal inwardness rather than to the public realm. These cults were emotionally charged and called for a personal choice and a personal commitment which had no direct bearing upon political life, and did not at any point challenge the claims of the official political religion. They fulfilled a different need – the longing for a personal and emotional relationship with a god – and nurtured different virtues from the public religion. The devotee approached his god as a person, not a citizen, and his worship neither impinged upon nor undercut his citizenship. These religions were sects in the sense that they related to the individual, the family and the small group, and made no attempt to address the broader society and its concerns. They were private in as far as they were voluntary: one chose one's cult, and the religion that was true for its devotees made no public, inspectable claims to being true for everyone. This duality between private and public, or political, religion was almost universally recognized. All citizens were expected to make some formal acknowledgement of the public religion, to burn a pinch of incense to the divine emperor and to refrain from open disparagement of the official cult; but in their private lives they were free to choose whatever form of worship touched their hearts, and to believe any religion that did not declare itself incompatible with the official cult.

Christianity spurned this dualism by laying claim to the heart without abandoning the public realm. It made claims which were universal and clearly incompatible with the official civil religion. For this faith the individual was more than a creature of the state, and found ultimate fulfilment not in the earthly city, but in the City of God. Others might give a formal assent to the public religion while finding their personal solace in a private and ecstatic cult or in the life of philosophy. But for the Christian this was not possible. Piety and patriotism were not the same thing. Christians were quickly seen as people of divided loyalties, precisely because they refused to evacuate the public realm, and regarded Christian theology as an exploration of the faith held by individuals which was at the same time a political theology inevitably in tension with the official theology of the state. The Christian faith claimed both to give a sense of meaning and significance to individuals and to sustain society.

There were not at first many resources to hand for the latter task. The early Church, as a small and powerless minority in a colonial context, believing that the present age was drawing rapidly to its close, did not concern itself to any great degree with political responsibilities. And when such matters became unavoidable, it was quickly found that New Testament, and distinctively Christian, teaching required to be supplemented from the Old Testament and from secular philosophy, particularly Stoicism and, to some extent, Neoplatonism. It was this kind of synthesis which underlay the development of 'Christendom'. In both its forms, the Byzantine and the Western, Christendom meant the definitive entry of Christianity into the public realm, there to fulfil functions unthought of in the early days of the Church. These went far beyond prayer for, and obedience to, the authorities, the demystification of power and the claim that the great central images of the Christian faith – the Kingdom, the Lord, the City, and so on – have a bearing on the public realm on earth. Now the Church itself was a powerful institution and was looked to for support and guidance by the rulers, who repeatedly saw it as the ideological wing of government and little more. Church leaders had to learn how to be chaplains to the powerful, not merely pastors of little flocks of the weak. But through the whole Christendom period – from Constantine till recent times – there was a serious and sustained endeavour to shape society on Christian principles, to seek in the Gospel guidance for rulers and to regulate the political and economic systems with criteria agreeable to the Christian faith. Thus there were developed sophisticated theories of the just war, the just price and the just wage, which began from the assumption that there exist in human nature an aggression and an acquisitiveness which are inherently sinful and must be curbed if something approaching a Christian social life is to be possible.

In the development of Christendom it was quickly discovered that not only did intellectual resources require to be borrowed from sources that were not explicitly Christian, but significant compromises had to be made. Although the Church and theology undoubtedly did something to moderate and control the capacity and bellicosity of the powerful, the price was a blessing of the established order of power and the introduction into Christian theology of major elements of old ways of thought about politics which sat very uneasily alongside the worship of a crucified God. At its best, Christendom was an exploration of a question which had not occurred in the early days of the Church: how may Christian rulers responsibly and piously use their power to the glory of God and the welfare of God's people? At its worst, it would appear that Christendom was not so much the 'establishment' of the Christian faith as its subversion.

THE REFORMATION AND THE FRAGMENTATION OF CHRISTENDOM

Whatever form Christendom might take, Christian faith and theology were always located near the centre of the public arena. Christian truth was open to public inspection and examination like any other truth: the law and the other institutions of society should be based on a Christian understanding of life; and society was entitled to godly (not merely just or educated) magistrates and a godly prince. Sometimes, religion became a formality which was a necessary expression of belonging to a community – at one and the same time the *corpus mysticum*, the mystical body of the Church, and the body politic, a declaration of patriotism, and a form of social control. Religions of the heart like the Cathari, the Franciscans, the Brethren of the Free Spirit and so forth, operated in the private arena, appealed to the emotions in a way 'official Christianity' sometimes did not and were usually suspect in the eyes of the institutional Church and of the state as well.

The Reformation made a renewed claim on the individual's heart. Justification is by faith, and no one can have faith for another. Luther (1483–1546) nurtured a passionate inwardness, and had a profound suspicion of religious institutions, only equalled by his reverence for secular power. The Church, he taught, is a fellowship gathered by the Lord and nourished on word and sacrament; its institutional structure is hardly important. Works righteousness, formalism, ritual, the outward – all these are to be radically questioned. Salvation is a matter of the restoration of the relationship with God and one's fellows, not a mechanism or an institutionalized procedure. The Gospel is addressed to the person, and it is the person who must respond. Particularly with Luther, but to an extent with the whole reformation movement, we find a major reaffirmation of the private realm, of inwardness, of the importance of the individual. Nothing can be more important than the destiny of each person, and the individual faith on which that destiny depends. It is not surprising that some recent historians have suggested that the Reformation and Counter-reformation formed the first time that the masses of Europe had been Christianized – by efforts to transform a formal respect for the Church and its teaching into a living personal faith based on an understanding of the content of Christianity.

Luther depoliticized the Christian faith. As the Church is not essentially an institution but a spiritual fellowship, he saw the whole medieval controversy between Pope and emperor as out of place. There are not two swords, as people had believed from the time of Pope Gelasius, but only one, and that is in the hands of the temporal power. The Church, provided it is free to preach and administer the sacraments, has no need for a separate jurisdiction, and its true function is distorted if it meddles in matters political. The private sphere is the proper arena of the Church's activity.

Yet God also rules in the public realm: Luther had no doubt about that. But here he rules in a different way, through different agents, Princes, magistrates, and all who hold public office behave according to reason, prudence and the great thinkers of the past, not in accordance with the Gospel. Aristotle, whom Luther dismissed as 'this damned, conceited, rascally heathen', when considering his influence in theology, becomes a reputable authority in the secular realm, where matters are based on reason rather than the Gospel:

> God made the secular government subject to reason because it is to have no jurisdiction over the welfare of souls or things of eternal value, but only over bodily and temporal goods, which God places under man's dominion. For this reason, nothing is taught in the Gospel about how it is to be maintained and regulated, except that the Gospel bids people honour it and not oppose it. Therefore the heathen can speak and teach about this very well, as they have done. And, to tell the truth, they are far more skillful in such matters than the Christians ... Whoever wants to learn and become wise in secular government, let him read the heathen books and writings.
>
> (Luther, AE XIII, p. 198)

The ruler, like others in their callings, acts as a representative of God, a mask or veil for God's work of love and justice in the world. Thus the statesman, in fulfilling his God-given vocation, is not infrequently obliged to do things that appear to be contrary to injunctions in, for instance, the Sermon on the Mount which, properly understood, apply only in the private or spiritual realm. Accordingly, when the ruler resorts to war or violence, 'The hand that wields this sword and slays with it is then no more man's hand but God's, who hangs, tortures, beheads, slays and fights. All these are His works and His judgements' (Luther, PE V, p. 36). The public realm is thus set free from Church and theological control, and Luther suggests that the whole political and social order is God-given and that rulers, even tyrants, are deputies of God. 'I might boast,' he wrote, 'that, since the Apostles' time the temporal sword and temporal government have never been so clearly described or so highly praised as by me' (Luther, PE V, p. 35). And herein lies the central problem; in affirming the autonomy under God of the temporal order, of the state, he seems to deny the possibility of a prophetic Christian assessment of the activity of the state, save such as is involved in boundary maintenance. Except in the event of the state transgressing into spiritual matters, the pious Lutheran is likely to be passively and uncritically obedient. In defending the autonomy under God of the secular realm in his 'two kingdoms' theory, Luther has not so much denied the possibility of a political theology as permitted a political theology which, like the old pagan political theologies, sacralizes the existing order alongside a Gospel effectively confined to the spiritual and private part of life. Luther's depoliticized Christian faith provides a strong implied legitimation of the status quo.

Calvin (1509–64) and his disciples shared with the Lutherans the conviction that in the medieval Church the Christian faith had been politicized so that the Church had become obsessed with secular power to the detriment of its proper work. The Gospel had been understood in legalistic terms, and the cultivation of the religion of the heart among the masses had been seriously neglected. But in other matters the Lutherans and Calvinists diverged markedly. Calvin and his followers had, it is true, a doctrine of the two kingdoms. Yet they did not separate them as sharply as did the Lutherans. There was among the Calvinists a peculiarly strong stress on the overarching sovereignty of God, as manifested in Jesus Christ. Luther made a sharp distinction between the 'right hand' and the 'left hand' of God, or God's 'proper' and his 'alien' work, so that sometimes it appeared that he believed that God operated in ways which were not simply different but opposed and conflicting. For Calvin, however, there must be a profound harmony in the workings of the divine sovereignty. Law and Gospel are not fundamentally opposed, and it is primarily through revelation that we come to know how God works in the world. The Calvinist tradition therefore makes possible a distinctively

Christian political theology which addresses the political order on the basis of revealed truth.

Furthermore, Calvin drew the frontier between the two realms at a different point. For him, the structure of the Church was not an indifferent matter which the civil authorities might arrange as seemed good to them, but something integrally related to the Gospel. The Church should be free not only to preach and celebrate the sacraments, but to order its own life in accordance with the Word of God, and maintain its freedom from secular control. The existence of the Church as a visible institution on earth is of profound theological significance.

The Reformation saw civil government in rather negative terms: it was a 'dyke against sin' or 'a remedy to vices'. While Luther was reluctant to be specific about how the state should restrain evil (that was not his task as a theologian), Calvin and his followers went into considerable detail, for they believed that Scripture lays down patterns of political behaviour and outlines the nature of fundamental social institutions such as marriage. Temporal government has been established 'to adapt our conduct to human society, to form our manners to civil justice, to conciliate us to each other, to cherish common peace and tranquillity' (Calvin, *Institutes* IV 20, p. 2). More specifically, the state is to care for the poor, erect schools and universities, maintain the peace, and establish justice (Calvin, *Letter to the King of England*, CR XIV, p. 40). Matters such as these are spiritually important, and it is a duty laid upon the Church and her leaders to remind the state of its responsibilities. In, for example, Scotland in the first century or so after the Reformation ministers were repeatedly enjoined to denounce from the pulpit the injustices and oppressions of the rich and powerful. This opens the way to theocracy: since the Word of God is the only sure guide in politics as in everything else, rulers and magistrates should expect to be guided, and perhaps rebuked, by the authorized interpreters of that Word. The Calvinists did not believe that they were politicizing the Gospel. In refusing to evacuate the realm of politics, they felt that they were being faithful to what they found in Scripture, and relating the private and the public in a way which was authentically Christian.

The so-called 'Radical Reformation', the enthusiasts and extreme sects so feared and denounced by the mainstream reformers, went further than the Calvinists in seeking to replace existing states with holy commonwealths which would be manifestations of the New Jerusalem, in which all would live by the Gospel and true Christian fellowship would replace coercion and inequality. They stood squarely in the tradition we have associated with the name of Tertullian. These utopian political theologies were profoundly millenarian and apocalyptic, and were correctly understood as posing a challenge to the whole established order. They did not take as seriously as those in the mainstream of the Reformation the limitations imposed on political activity in a fallen world. But they posed a challenge to the compromises and conservatism characteristic of most Reformation political thought.

Various factors encouraged a theological evacuation of the public realm in the centuries after the Reformation. Lutheranism naturally developed into a pietism which taught political passivity. Calvinism and the radical sects both developed theocratic emphases which often refused to recognize a degree of autonomy in the political order. The Reformation and the ensuing wars of religion fragmented Europe and convinced many people that Christianity was inherently divisive. If states were to maintain peace and establish justice, it seemed that the principles of politics must be looked for elsewhere than in warring theologies and a shattered, bickering Church. In order to do its job, politics must be emancipated from religion. And, as R. H. Tawney showed in his classic study, *Religion and the Rise of Capitalism*, theology withdrew, almost with relief, from the increasing complexities of the public realm because it had come to believe that 'it is in the heart of the individual that religion has its throne, and to externalize it in rules and institutions is to tarnish its purity and to degrade its appeal' (Tawney, 1926, p. 280).

THE ENLIGHTENMENT AND THE OMNIPOTENCE OF REASON

The fragmentation of Christendom was certainly not a conscious intention of the Reformation. All the protagonists in the struggle maintained a hope for a restored Christendom, based on a renewed and purified theology, and grounded on Christian assumptions. If, as we have seen, many of the reformers strove for the emancipation of politics from constant ecclesiastical tutelage, it was for the sake of the purity of the faith and the integrity of the political realm, not because they were reluctantly compelled to retreat from territory that they believed was properly theirs. And, at most, they argued only for a relative autonomy under God for politics. They would have been horrified at the notion that theology should have nothing to say about political or economic life. R. H. Tawney puts the point forcefully: 'To the most representative minds of the Reformation, as of the Middle Ages, a philosophy which treated the transactions of commerce and the institutions of society as indifferent to religion would have appeared, not merely morally reprehensible, but intellectually absurd' (Tawney, 1926, p. 279).

It was the eighteenth-century Enlightenment, not the Reformation, which declared the sovereignty of the reason, free from any dogmatic presuppositions or religious guidance. 'Enlightenment,' Kant (1724–1804) declared, 'is man's leaving his self-caused immaturity. Maturity is the capacity to use one's intelligence without the guidance of another ... *Sapere Aude*! Have the courage to use your own intelligence! is therefore the motto of the Enlightenment' (Kant, 1949 edn, p. 132). This liberation depended upon the establishment of a new framework of thought, and new rational criteria for thinking. Doubt, questioning, the interrogation of reality and the torturing of nature to make her reveal her secrets were the foundation of the new enterprise, as they had been of Socratic thought centuries before. Religion and theology, like everything else, were now called to account for themselves at the bar of reason, and not surprisingly a system which cast a sceptical eye on all inherited and traditional assumptions about truth and goodness tended increasingly frequently to regard religion as a private option arising from arbitrary and irrational choices. Christianity became one instance of the class 'religion', rather than the basic assumption of the culture. Belief, faith, dogma were regarded with curiosity or suspicion as private choices without public relevance. And the most convincing apologists, defending Christianity against 'its cultured despisers', took it for granted that religion was a matter for the heart and not for public life. Thus, Schleiermacher (1768–1834) saw theology as the exploration of the religious consciousness, and Kierkegaard (1813–55) proclaimed that truth is to be found in subjectivity. They and their like did not, and could not, produce an understanding of Christianity which was, in any significant way, prophetic. Kierkegaard's occasional forays into the public realm, such as his celebrated *Attack on Christendom*, must be understood as endeavours to rescue a private and passionate faith from the dilution and compromise involved in faith finding an institutional expression. It was not that the Enlightenment was against religion; it supported religion on condition that it kept to its own narrowly circumscribed place. It was more positively disposed towards a general rational religion of reason (Kant's 'Religion within the Limits of Reason Alone'), which applied to human beings as such, than towards a specific religion like Christianity with its exclusive and universal claims.

This natural religion of the Enlightenment has profoundly influenced Christianity's self-understanding. It is, according to Metz, despite its claim to apply to all human beings:

> as elitist as the enlightened reason itself. It is in fact only applicable to the new man of the Enlightenment, the citizen, as the subject of reason. The natural religion, then, is an extremely privatized religion that has been, as it were, specially prepared for the domestic use of the propertied middle class citizen. It is above all a religion of inner feeling. It does not protest against or oppose in any way the definitions of reality, meaning and truth, for example, that are accepted by the middle class society of exchange and success. It gives greater height and depth to what already applies even without it.
>
> (Metz, 1980, p. 45)

Christianity has cheerfully allowed itself to become domesticated within the private, middle-class domain. There it is comfortable and appreciated – on condition that it keeps to its new limits, asks no awkward questions and does not obtrude the disturbing memories of the Son of God, condemned and executed by the political authorities and rejected by the religion and culture of his day. Christianity has won a Pyrrhic victory over the Enlightenment, argues Metz: post-Enlightenment Christianity, willingly confined to the middle-class domestic sphere, subtly legitimates the established order to which it has unknowingly capitulated.

The privatization of religion involved the emancipation of the polity and the economy from theological control. The argument of Carl Becker that the thinkers of the Enlightenment 'demolished the Heavenly City of St Augustine only to rebuild it with more up-to-date materials' (Becker, 1932, p. 31) is only partly true. Augustine's City must indeed be disposed of, because Augustine's understanding of history as the sphere of God's gracious activity is no longer acceptable. The tension that is central to Augustine's thought between what is possible in the earthly city and the promise and hope of the City of God is almost entirely lost, and in consequence people are taught to be fully at home in the earthly city.

But social and economic institutions are not regarded simply as devices made to serve the purposes of human beings. The market, the political order, and the class ranking of society are 'given' (by whom it is not clear) and acquire a strange quality of secularized sacredness. They are to be approached with reverence; their origin is mysterious, and it is as dangerous to tamper with them as it was to interfere with the ark of God. The 'hidden hand' of Adam Smith (1723–90) ensures that private selfishness is transubstantiated into the common good, and discourages people from asking whose are the hands behind the hidden hand. Hegel's (1770–1831) 'cunning of reason' is another numinous phrase, capable of eliciting a quasi-religious awe which inhibits the asking of awkward questions. A kind of secular idolatry of the established order of things in culture and society, combined with rigorous questioning in other areas, was characteristic of the Enlightenment. This goes far beyond the autonomy that Luther allocated to the secular sphere. A prophetic understanding of the Christian faith was virtually suppressed.

SECULARIZATION AND PLURALISM

Secularization and the development of pluralism provide further explanation of the collapse of Christendom and the relegation of Christianity to the sphere of the private. We are not here concerned with the detail of the debate among sociologists about the nature, impact and significance of secularization. It is enough to register that the process is one of the decline of the influence of institutional religion and of religious observance, a development which appears to be closely associated with modernity. The Christendom model fitted a more simple, face-to-face society; urban, industrial, mass society provides a less congenial setting for the traditional forms of organized religion. Mary Douglas argues that the secular person is 'an age-old cosmological type, which need have nothing to do with urban life or modern science' (Douglas, 1970, p. 36). But, having firmly and properly knocked on the head the romantic notion that 'primitive man is by nature deeply religious', she then proceeds to acknowledge that in modern society, with its emphasis on individual freedom, its vast and formless social conglomerations and its impersonal types of communication, traditional churchly expressions of religion have a hard time of it. It is not, of course, that religion *as such* has been erased by secularization. Sects, operating on the margins, frequently flourish exceedingly; the practices known today by the sociologists as 'implicit religion' are amazingly widespread; astrology and the occult attract at least as much attention as ever; media evangelists conduct operations which in scale and turnover rival some significant corporations and, paradoxically, deny their 'evangelical' label by suggesting powerfully that salvation or healing can be bought. This last is a reminder that in some situations, which are emphatically 'modern', urban and industrial, organized religion, even 'old time religion', flourishes but in a form which is itself, it is argued, thoroughly secularized and reflects and reinforces the values and procedures of secular society. The growth of fundamentalist politics and the New Christian Right might give us pause, but even when all allowances have been made and every appropriate qualification entered, it is in general true that in

most modern societies institutional religion plays a less significant role than it did in the past, and commonly sees its
function in the public arena primarily as defending traditional
standards of personal morality.

How is this development to be interpreted theologically? In
the twentieth century theology has made strenuous and varied
efforts to understand and respond to the processes of secularization and the growth of pluralism. It has been recognized
that this is necessary if theology is to remain in any real sense in
the public realm. Friedrich Gogarten argues that the world has
been secularized by God in Jesus Christ. This means that it is
not appropriate to approach it with a religious veneration; the
world is set free to *be* the world. It no longer requires to be sacralized. Gogarten is a Lutheran, who operates with the two
kingdoms doctrine, and endeavours to ground his thinking
upon justification by faith alone. He sees a sharp disjunction
between Gospel and law, faith and works, God and the world,
salvation history and 'ordinary' history. No activity in the
world can earn salvation, and the recognition that the world is
the sphere of love, not faith, sets us free to take the world and
our neighbour seriously in themselves, without reference to our
salvation. God has made human beings adult and responsible
heirs in the world, free to relate the God in faith and to love the
neighbour and the world for their own sake, not as the currency
of salvation. Accordingly, Gogarten sees secularization as the
outworking of the Christian faith, which puts faith where it
belongs, and where alone it may be authentic – in the private,
inward sphere. It does not generate a worldview or an ethic, let
alone an ideology or a philosophical system; indeed, it emanci-
pates the believer to deal lovingly as a responsible adult with
the world. But what he calls *secularism*, the attempt to reduce
Christian faith to a system of contemporary ideas, the politicization of Christianity, introduced fatal distortions in the way
both the world and the faith are understood (Shiner, 1966;
Davis, 1980, p. 36ff).

Dietrich Bonhoeffer appears on the face of it to hold a position
strikingly similar to Gogarten's, although it is relevant to
remember that while Gogarten flirted with the 'German
Christians' and at one stage seemed to find their views

compatible with his, Bonhoeffer steadfastly struggled against
Nazism and Hitler. In Bonhoeffer we find a particularly notable
and influential acceptance of a world that has 'come of age',
together with an affirmation of secularization – ruling totally
out of court any theological nostalgia for Christendom, indeed
for 'religion' – combined in the conviction that the Christian
'must live a "worldly" life and so participate in the suffering of
God' (Bonhoeffer, 1956, p. 166). For Bonhoeffer this 'worldly'
lifestyle meant political involvement and commitment to the
struggle against Nazism, and finally complicity in the plot to
assassinate Hitler, which led to his arrest and execution. This
posed particularly acute problems to a conscience shaped by the
Lutheran tradition. Bonhoeffer's affirmation of the secular was
in no sense triumphalistic; he did not see secularization as the
construction of the City of God, or as a modern way of speaking
of salvation history. Demonic forces such as Nazism still
flourish in a secular world, and it is there that they must be
confronted head on. Indeed, in struggling against oppression
and evil in the secular world – and in a Church which seemed all
but taken over by the world – Bonhoeffer discovered something
crucial which is not to be found in Gogarten's more detached
and formal theology of the secular: that in the secular world the
place of the Christian is alongside the poor and the weak, who
are still oppressed and forgotten by those who have 'come of
age': 'It is an experience of incomparable value to have learned
to see the great events of the history of the world from beneath:
from the viewpoint of the useless, the suspect, the abused, the
powerless, the oppressed, the despised – in a word, from the
viewpoint of those who suffer' (quoted in Gutierrez, 1983,
p. 231).

This emphasis lay largely unexplored by those who saw
themselves as the heirs of Bonhoeffer. Instead, they pressed
forward in the 1960s with a theology which affirmed and indeed
celebrated the secular and accepted modernity without
significant reservations. Harvey Cox's paean of praise for *The
Secular City* (1965) regarded it as the fruit of a God-given
process of secularization which presented new opportunities of
freedom, maturity and responsibility. Arendt Th. van Leeuwen
developed with great erudition the thesis that the world wide

spread of secularism and Western technology was a continuation and culmination of the Christian world mission (van Leeuwen, 1964). Denys Munby in his *The Idea of a Secular Society* (1963) called on Christians to embrace the values of a secular society. This style of theology, with a few notable exceptions in Bonhoeffer and Ronald Gregor Smith, seems in retrospect too easy an accommodation to the Spirit of the Age, singularly lacking in critical edge and prophetic questioning. The panegyrics for secularization for the most part forgot, what Bonhoeffer could never overlook, that a secular society may be diabolic, idolatrous and exploitative, and that people who have come of age do not cease thereby to be sinners. The secular theologies of the 1960s did not withdraw from the public realm, or cease to ask questions about what God was doing in history, or deny the spiritual significance of the social and political order. They attempted a theological interpretation of their time, yet ended with a Eusebian sanctification of the secular, and a celebration of the secular city which amounted in the political sphere at least to little more than reflection and endorsement of the superficial optimism of the day.

Such theologies were quite incapable of taking the measure of the secular human being who exploits his neighbour and destroys his environment. They could not understand that the secularization which was experienced as emancipation by some was simultaneously felt as oppression by others, who saw theologies of the secular as justifications of oppression. All the theologies of the secular except those of Bonhoeffer and his close associates were radically politicized in the sense that they argued that theology had a proper place in the public realm but in fact did little but reflect and reinforce the conventional wisdom and the dominant ideologies of the modern world. Van Leeuwen, for example, reduces the mission of the Church to the aggressive spread of secularization and Western technological culture throughout the world, so that theology becomes no more than a supporting ideology which cannot assess or criticize the one-dimensional world of modern technology. Van Leeuwen is a Calvinist; the Lutheran Gogarten must take a different route to a similar destination. By affirming that faith belongs emphatically in the private or individual sphere,

Gogarten is not only making a traditionally Lutheran statement but also expressing the usual understanding of the place of religion in modern Western society – it is a personal, domestic, subjective matter. Faith gives no guidance, or defence against ideological imperialism in the public realm. Charles Davis's judgement is a fair one: 'All that Gogarten would seem to have done is to have translated the attitudes and values of contemporary society into theological jargon' (Davis, 1980, p. 43).

There are modern secular societies which are not pluralist, in the sense that they have one dominant ideology or political theology (even if in some cases an atheistic one), usually supported by a cultic pattern to which a large proportion of the people owe some kind of allegiance. The Soviet Union, with its elaborate development of Marxist–Leninist ritual to complement the 'establishment' of Marxism–Leninism as the official ideology of the state, is a case in point (Lane, 1981).

This reminds us that secularism and pluralism are not the same thing and a theological response to pluralism may be very different from a theology that attempts to interpret secularization. Pluralism implies diversity of values, opinions, interests and insights, as well as religious allegiance. The key question posed classically by Durkheim (1858–1917) is about what holds together a plural society. Communist and other totalitarian states in the modern world seek social cohesion through the imposition of an ideology, and are savage in their treatment of dissidents, as were the states of Christendom in the past in their treatment of heretics and their attempts to enforce orthodoxy. But is a *totally* pluralistic society possible? A society, that is, in which there is no consensus whatever on values or views of the world, in which no opinions are excluded or disallowed? We may accept John Habgood's argument that in a pluralistic nation, although there is no one dominant or generally accepted ideology or world view, there must be enough agreement on values, goals and underlying assumptions to 'hold the nation together', to give some basic sense of national identity and to authorize the continuing debate about policies, objectives and the welfare of the community. A radically pluralistic society with a state that is entirely neutral on basic questions is unthinkable; there has to be some minimum consensus to provide the necessary degree of coherence. Habgood is probably right also in suggesting that periods of crisis bring to the surface the consensual basis which exists even in avowedly pluralistic societies, and of which people for much of the time are unaware. In time of war, for instance, the churches, otherwise regarded as marginal, find themselves moved towards the centre of the stage (Habgood, 1983, pp. 28ff). A major role of the Church, it is argued, has been to lay down the foundations of this consensus, to implant gradually over many centuries values and attitudes which are now often viewed as separate from the Christian faith, and to sustain the consensual basis for national life. This surely is a contribution of the Christian faith to the public sphere in a pluralistic nation which is of importance. But it is only part of the total contribution that may properly be expected. As well as implanting specific values and assessing particular policies in the light of faith, in addition to the care of the victims and the disturbing support of the decision-makers, there is also a need for a prophetic social critique which arises out of identification with the power-less. But to make any of these contributions, it is necessary first to resist the relegation of religion to the private sphere which is so characteristic of pluralistic societies. The other great danger is to allow the reduction of Christianity to the proportions of a formal and ceremonial civil religion operating in a syncretistic and tolerant context reminiscent of the late Roman Empire.

THE POLITICIZATION DEBATE

The theory that religion belongs in inwardness and private life – that it has no place in the public arena – has, as we have seen, a long history. And, of course, even a private religion can be 'useful' politically, can powerfully affirm the established order of things without appearing to say anything directly about politics. As Metz and Newbigin have argued so forcefully, Christianity in the Western world has in large part entered happily into a cheerful domesticity in which it subtly legitimates the existing order (Newbigin, 1983). Politicization – understanding the Christian faith primarily in terms of its political relevance and its public role – also has a history, as we saw in chapter 1. The theology of Eusebius is the paradigm of politicized Christianity. And some contemporary commentators accuse Christianity, not of being domesticated and private, but of politicizing faith as a desperate and self-destructive response to secularization and Church decline.

An influential development of the charge of politicization came in the 1979 BBC Reith Lectures by Dr Edward Norman, the Dean of Peterhouse, Cambridge, later published as *Christianity and the World Order* (Norman, 1979). Norman understands politicization as the reduction of the Christian faith to secular idealism. 'Christianity today', he writes, 'is being reinterpreted as a scheme of social and political action, dependent, it is true, upon supernatural authority for its ultimate claims to attention, but rendered in categories which are derived from the political theories and practices of contemporary society' (Norman, 1979, p. 2). The content of Christianity is being changed, so that it reflects and reinforces the modern obsession with politics, and the mistaken belief that every problem is capable of a political solution. Thus, the Gospel is transformed from being a message of eternal hope for the individual into a programme for solving the world's problems; political goals and purposes are substituted for religious ones, and human destiny is understood in exclusively this-worldly terms. The Church in its concerns, pronouncements and activities becomes almost indistinguishable from a political party. Theology, or what passes for theology, is hardly more than a reflection of the passing fashions of the day, loosely related to Marxism and expressing in superficially Christian terms the ideals and expectations of bourgeois liberalism. The social teaching of the Church has simply been borrowed from the secular, left-wing intelligentsia and is remarkably detached from any respect for the enduring Christian concerns for eternity and for the individual. This 'internal transformation of the faith itself so that it comes to be defined in social values' leads Norman to ask: 'What will happen to Christianity as its

content is drained away into the great pool of secular idealism?'
(Norman, 1979, p. 13). This wishy-washy reflection of secular
idealism that has replaced the Gospel has, moreover, been
exported by expatriate clergy and a Westernized elite of Church
leaders to the Third World, where it will inevitably sap spiritual
vitality as it has already done in the West. This is the true origin
of liberation theology – one of Norman's main targets. These
articulate and radical Church leaders are not the true voice of
the poor and the oppressed, but represent the prejudices and
views they have imbibed in Western or Western-style universities and seminaries. The politicization of the Third World
churches is yet another instance of Western cultural
imperialism.

At its heart, Norman believes, Christianity is not so much
concerned with ethics and politics as with 'the ethereal qualities
of immortality' (misprinted in the original version in *The
Listener* as 'the ethereal qualities of *immorality*'!). Authentic
Christianity, he argues, is about human fallibility, about the
worthlessness of all earthly expectations. It is profoundly pessimistic about worldly existence and, in particular, about
attempts to improve the human lot. No political project is
capable of inaugurating a just society, for human nature is
corrupt and we live in a fallen world, where the only politics that
is worth taking seriously is the politics of imperfection.

We should note here that Norman is not in fact suggesting
that Christians can be abstracted from politics entirely. He
seems to believe that the Church as an institution should be
extremely cautious about political involvement, but that
individual Christians may, or should, undertake political
activity in a chastened way, acutely aware of the limits of
politics:

> In the world, the Christian seeks to apply the great love of God
> as well as he can in contemporary terms. And that will actually
> involve corporate social and political action. But unlike the
> secular moralizers whom the Christian activists of the present
> day so closely resemble, the wise aspirant to eternity will
> recognize no hope of a better social order in his endeavours, for he
> knows that the expectations of men are incapable of satisfaction.

Before even the goal of one generation is achieved, another sets other goals.

(Norman, 1979, p. 79)

True Christianity is thus essentially private and personal. And the application of 'the great love of God' is by way of personal or collective charity rather than engagement with the structures of society. Since no human society can be perfect, power is best left in the hands of responsible and prudent people and if they are Christians, so much the better. It is in this way, rather than through pronouncements of prelates or synods, that Christianity influences politics (Hinchliff in Willmer, 1979, pp. 17–18).

Norman's critique is at the same time a very useful corrective to some fashionable distortions of the relation of Christianity and politics, and a colossal misunderstanding of what is happening in the world Church. It is true that the Gospel is sometimes presented as a political programme *simpliciter*. But to focus on such aberrations, as Norman does, runs the danger of making prosperous Western Christians singularly complacent in face of the poverty and hunger of the world, and blinds them to the importance and the challenge of the contemporary rediscovery of the centrality of justice in the Christian scheme of things. Norman commends a seductive truncated version of Christianity which is at least as unbalanced on the other side as the 'politicized Christianity' he attacks. In the contemporary ecumenical encounter with the pain, hunger and oppression of the world there is to be found a renovation and clarification of the Gospel which is of far greater importance than the accompanying stupidities and distortions (Forrester in Willmer, 1979, pp. 34–46). Norman encourages Western Christians to return to their dogmatic slumbers, unwilling to face the challenges and opportunities presented by the new ecumenism in its engagement with the Gospel and the problems of the world, and unable to see that the Spirit is at work and the devil does not have it all his own way. Kwame Nkrumah's slogan, 'Seek ye first the political kingdom', was engraved on his statue which stood in Accra while he was in power. Norman is right that this is heresy; only it is not the motto of most of those he castigates. They take seriously what he does not: that disciples are bidden to seek first the Kingdom of God and accordingly cannot, in Barth's words, be 'indifferent or neutral towards the political structures of this world which are so clearly related to [the Church's] own mission' (Barth, 1954, p. 22).

Norman is a church historian, not a theologian. Neither in *Christianity and the World Order* nor elsewhere does he develop his own theological position in any detail. The sixth Reith Lecture, on 'The Indwelling Christ' is the nearest he comes to expounding a theology. Here he repeats his warnings against indentifying the Christian faith with the secular values of the age, and his charge that the theologians and Church leaders have lost confidence in the uniqueness of the Christian revelation and are engaged in reformulating Christianity to make it compatible with, and a reflection of, contemporary moral enthusiasms. As against this urge to expound the political relevance of Christianity, Dr Norman says, 'True religion points to the condition of the inward soul of man.' In place of the politicized optimism he denounces he puts a cynicism about human nature and human capabilities: 'Human beings are rubbish.' And at the heart of the Christian religion, he argues, stands a Christ, who rejected the official politicized religion of his day and called on people to abandon worldly concerns and enter a Kingdom which is not of this world and is entered only by those who are born again. Christ, he says, had 'a sense of the worthlessness of human values' which approximates to what he calls' historical relativism' (Norman, 1979, p. 82). A rediscovery of this sense of historical relativism is the most important task facing the Church, for only so may a proper sense of the contingency of human values be combined with belief in the absoluteness of Christianity.

To explore further the theological underpinning of E. R. Norman's conclusions one has to turn elsewhere. Norman is an Anglican, and like many Anglicans, he tends to fall back on characteristically Lutheran modes of thought, particularly perhaps in social theology. Indeed, Norman's position is really only intelligible in the framework of a two kingdoms theory. He is also an Anglican who takes the responsibilities and opportunities of establishment very seriously, and is regarded as an acceptable theologian by the British New Right. His attack on the politicization of Christianity is perfectly compatible with according theological legitimation to right-wing views, and he sees the model of the politicization of the Church represented by the establishment of the Church of England as acceptable. We will explore these matters with special reference to a recent book by a Dutch Calvinist (who writes like a Lutheran) H. M. Kuitert, *Everything is Politics but Politics is not Everything – A Theological Perspective on Faith and Politics*, and to some writing by Roger Scruton, the conservative philosopher.

Kuitert starts from the very proper and necessary affirmation that there is more to Christianity than political action and that a great deal of political action benefits from being detached from religious or theological control. For him, theology is not social theory or criticism of the political and economic orders, but examination and criticism of the 'outline proclamation' of the Church. It is about the Gospel and eternal salvation, not primarily about earthly flourishing. Kuitert has what might be called a 'purist' understanding of theology: it is narrowly focused on the message of salvation, on the Christian Gospel, which, he believes, does not in fact generate any political directives; when Christians claim to be deriving political guidance from the Gospel, or speaking of the political implications of the Gospel, they are simply attempting to give a Christian aura to injunctions which are in fact based on some secular theory. The common left-wing understanding of the relationship of the Gospel and ethics does not find support in traditional Christian political philosophy and ethics, which are, Kuitert argues, inherently conservative: 'Religious faith, including Christian faith, does not just have a conservative effect but is also by nature conservative when it comes to relations with society' (Kuitert, 1986, p. 38). However, he continues: 'Religious faith seems to be not only the mirror of a society; it can also create conditions for not coinciding with it as an individual. In this way religious faith can be a window as well as a mirror: it keeps open the sense that society should be different. Thus, in times of crisis, religion can become a breeding

ground for the self-criticism of a society' (Kuitert, 1986, p. 55).
But religion on its own cannot carry through this self-criticism,
because 'criticism needs criteria, and criteria for the social and
political order do not come from religious faith (Kuitert, 1986,
p. 55).

Kuitert identifies Karl Barth as being responsible for most of
the defects he identifies in modern political theology, because
Barth believed that theology was more than an 'academic, professional discipline' concerned with an 'outline proclamation'
which does not engage directly with contemporary political
reality. For Barth, theology does indeed stimulate social
criticism and provide the criteria for this criticism; a Church
theology must judge and discern particular political policies,
realities and practices against its knowledge of the Lord of
Church and state. And Barth goes on:

> The Christian Church that is aware of its political responsibility
> will demand political preaching; and it will interpret it politically
> even if it contains no direct reference to politics. Let the church
> concentrate first, however, on seeing that the whole gospel really
> is preached within its own area. Then there will be no danger of
> the wider sphere beyond the Church not being wholesomely
> disturbed by it.
>
> (Barth, 1954, p. 47)

For Barth every dogmatic statement, every statement of faith,
also has ethical and political content; there is no absolute
separation between the indicative and imperative. And the
Gospel, and the theology which explore the Gospel, is concerned
with the *whole* of life, not just with a part.

It is precisely at this point that Kuitert has difficulties. If
Barth is right about the Gospel and about the nature of
theology, then 'theology is in principle saddled with all human
questions, including questions relating to social and political
action' (Kuitert, 1986, p. 26). But these questions are, Kuitert
believes, beyond the competence of the theologian *qua*
theologian; all he can say is either repetition of what others with
more knowledge of these matters have already said or is so
general as to be useless. There is no distinctive theological
contribution to be made, for 'the theological faculty does not

provide any insight into all these areas' (Kuitert, 1986, p. 26).
The Church as an institution should not be engaged in politics;
for it to be involved in struggles about power fundamentally
compromises its integrity. But individual Christians may, or
must, involve themselves in the political scene, aware that they
should look for guidance elsewhere than to the Church or to
theology.

For Kuitert, Barth is wrong in rejecting a doctrine of the two
kingdoms. He argues that basic political principles cannot and
need not be derived from the Gospel because they are already
there in the secular realm; they are not the fruit of the Word of
God but are accessible to everyone through reason independently of faith. One does not need to be a Christian to know what
good action is. Politics, in short, belongs in the secular realm;
theology, salvation and the Church are of the spiritual realm.
The two must never be confused; boundaries must be maintained. But Barth rejected the doctrine of the two kingdoms
advisedly. He had seen again and again – and not only in
relation to Nazism – how in the political sphere the real issue
had been idolatry versus faithfulness to God. He had seen how
confidence in rationality and the inherent decency of human
beings had been incapable of offering effective resistance to
demonic attacks on the Jews and on the Christian faith. He had
seen how many Lutherans were trained by their two kingdoms
doctrine into a political passivity which became in effect
collusion with Nazism. And he had looked closely at the New
Testament, and found there no trace of the kind of two
kingdoms theory developed by Luther and now reaffirmed by
Kuitert, as he explains in his book *Rechtfertigung und Recht*, in
English, *Church and State* (Barth, 1939). Here Barth presents
an extraordinarily thorough exegetical demonstration that the
New Testament knows nothing of two kingdoms as understood
in the Lutheran tradition. Kuitert's position would be more
impressive if he had taken account of this kind of argument. As
it is, it is remarkable how little biblical or doctrinal evidence he
presents to back up his conclusions. His crucial arguments are
in fact sociological rather than theological, and relate to the
nature and function of religion rather than to the distinctive
emphases of the Christian faith.

Barth and his disciples, says Kuitert, are responsible for the modern politicization of the Church, because they taught that all knowledge of God is to be found in the Word of God, Jesus Christ, and not elsewhere. This Word is preached and believed within the Church. Hence, it is within the Church that we are to look for a distinctive insight into God's will for the social and political order; the Church has a special unavoidable responsibility to and for the state. For Kuitert, this position involves a grossly inflated understanding of the Church, and of theology. They believe and proclaim the Word of God but, Kuitert argues, this does not mean that they have the answers to complex economic and political questions. They cannot solve the problem of defence and disarmament, for instance – who can? Put this way, Kuitert's point is valid. But his further suggestion that this implies that the Church and theology have no distinctive and important contribution to make to the discussion of such issues is false and encourages a dangerous withdrawal from the public realm, leaving the public square empty (to borrow Richard Neuhaus's phrase) and ready for seven devils to enter in. Politicization is the ruin of the Church, Kuitert says, because it makes the Church untrue to itself, an institution like any other, involved in the power games of the world. It undertakes a role for which it is totally and necessarily unequipped. It is impossible for the Church or for Church leaders in the modern world to be prophetic: 'What the Church thinks it has to say about politics is . . . so general that it does not amount to anything, or it is something that has already been said elsewhere' (Kuitert, 1986, p. 147).

It is possible to take seriously Kuitert's cautionary remarks while rejecting the view of theology and the Church which he presents. The Church visible cannot but be an institution, and institutions relate to other institutions and to people in terms of power. This is an unavoidable fact about the Church which is at once its glory, its danger and its responsibility. It cannot be wished away, and must not be forgotten or the whole understanding of the Church and its function in society is distorted.

E. R. Norman, on the other hand, appears to take the Church as a visible institution very seriously and accepts, along with other Anglicans such as John Habgood (Habgood, 1983) and

David Martin (Martin, 1980, 1981), that there is much to be said for an establishment such as that of the Church of England. This, it appears, is a proper and acceptable form of politicization, in which the Church plays the role of a civil religion, at some cost, perhaps, to a 'sectarian' understanding of Christianity and to ecumenical and transnational elements. Church leaders become chaplains to the powerful, and the Church is expected to provide both a general legitimation of the political order and a ritual celebration of the high points in national life. The Church of England, as David Martin has repeatedly emphasized, is virtually indistinguishable from the folk religion of the English people, and should gladly accept this inherently conservative role of implanting values and providing a sacral context for the sustaining of community life.

This form of politicization of the Church has been ably expounded and defended by a secular philosopher, Roger Scruton, in a book, *The Meaning of Conservatism*, which he interestingly calls a 'dogmatics of conservatism' (Scruton, 1980, pp. 11, 43). The state, he argues, must be sustained by something beyond politics, something that at least appears to be transcendent and gives to the state and its civil rituals an aura, relating the political and cosmic orders by way of myth and cult in a way quite close to that which we have seen so central in the ancient world:

> All ceremony requires a symbolic depth ... a sense that it reaches below the suface of things, and touches upon realities which cannot be translated into words ... The emotions which attach themselves to the ceremonies of state constantly outrun the objects which occasion them. Participant and observer find themselves taken up into something greater, of which the reality of military or political power is no more than a pale reflection. Thus there emerges the myth of the 'glory' of the nation, the myth of its absolute unqualified *right* to allegiance.
>
> (Scruton, 1980, p. 169)

There is, Scruton argues, a close link between belief in a transcendent bond and belief in a transcendent Being who upholds it. This inherently conservative belief has in Europe traditionally been understood in Christian terms and expressed in some form of establishment of the Christian Church and a commitment to 'the idea of a Christian society'. Even today the Church 'continues to provide the major institutions which reinforce the attachment of the citizen to the forms of civil life, and which turn his attention away from himself as individual, towards himself as social being' (Scruton, 1980, pp. 171–2). The Church is an institution which is itself necessarily political, and has as a major function the provision of a transcendent framework within which political activity may be properly understood and undertaken. However, the leadership of the churches has, Scruton argues, 'begun to set itself against the order of European society' (Scruton, 1980, p. 173); it has abdicated its traditional authority and role by advocating all sorts of radical secular causes. The Church must be saved from its leaders and from sectarian deviations if it is to become once again politically central, for 'the place of the church is either at the heart of things, or nowhere' (Scruton, 1980, p. 173). And establishment holds it to its task.

We thus seem to be dealing with two forms of politicization, not one. There is the form which both Norman and Kuitert denounce, which may be characterized as radical, left wing, ecumenical and sometimes sectarian, and there is the establishment model of politicization, which Norman accepts but of which Kuitert is (I think) suspicious, in which Christianity performs the functions of a civil religion, accepts a generally conservative role, and which may be regarded as right wing. If I am right that Kuitert rejects both kinds of politicization, he certainly does so on theological grounds. Furthermore he, unlike Norman, recognizes and engages with the theological roots of 'left-wing politicization'. What then is the theology of 'establishment politicization? It is perhaps significant that the arguments in such an intelligent and sophisticated defence of establishment politicization as John Habgood's *Church and Nation in a Secular Age* (1983) are almost all sociological rather than theological. One can, in other words, justify the establishment model in terms of the responsibilities and opportunities it presents, but it is more difficult to defend it in the categories of ecclesiology. The most cogent contemporary apologia for the establishment model that I know is that of Roger Scruton, and he argues in entirely secular and untheological terms.

What Scruton, Habgood and Norman do not seem to face is the possibility that Christianity is inherently a bad civil religion, and that to force it into this mould is corrosive of its Christian identity. Machiavelli (1469–1527) long ago realized that Christianity is an inferior civil religion because it divides people's loyalty, makes them question the edicts of the rulers and inculcates what Nietzsche (1844–1900) later called a 'slave morality' rather than the heroic virtues which strengthen the state. Because Christianity makes politics relative, Christians do not make good citizens and a Christian state is not a strong state. But religion is necessary to the state: 'Where the fear of God is wanting, there the country will come to ruin, unless it is sustained by the fear of the prince, which may *temporarily* supply the want of religion' (Machiavelli, 1950 edn, pp. 145–9). Religion keeps people 'well conducted and united' if it is 'judiciously used' by the rulers, who may well believe that this useful religion is false (Machiavelli, 1950 edn, pp. 149–53). The religion of ancient Rome, Machiavelli believed, was a truly heroic and effective civil religion; it would be politically advantageous were it to be restored. But, as a realistic man, Machiavelli considered ways in which Christianity might be useful for political purposes. In other words, he proposed a politicization of Christianity aware that this was a perversion of Christianity. Rousseau, (1712–78) too, believed that 'no state was ever yet founded save on a basis of religion', but Christianity, unlike other religions, is 'fundamentally more harmful than useful to the firm establishment of the community'. This is because when 'Jesus established on earth a Kingdom of the Spirit . . . a schism developed between the theological and the political system and . . . the State ceased to be one and indivisible, and developed the domestic divisions which have never ceased to disturb Christian Peoples' (Rousseau, 1947 edn, pp. 422–40).

If it is in fact correct that the nature of Christianity makes it an indifferent civil religion, might this perhaps be a hint that its distinctive service to the political order lies neither in withdrawal nor in immersion, whether to the Left or to the Right?

Christianity cannot be reduced to the dimensions of a religion of pious subjectivity or a religion of public policy. It is both – and more.

In a secular age it has become common on the part of Western Christians to look back longingly to the attempts to revive a rather romanticized version of medieval society, or Christendom, with ringing pronouncements such as this:

> The Christian can be satisfied with nothing less than a Christian organization of society – which is not the same thing as a society consisting exclusively of devout Christians. It would be a society in which the natural end of man – virtue and well-being in community – is acknowledged for all, and the supernatural end – beatitude – for those who have the eyes to see it.
>
> (Eliot, 1939, p. 34)

But if that kind of political theology has had its day with the recognition that Christendom has passed away beyond recall, there remains an urgent need for a post-Christendom political theology, more akin presumably to Augustine or Tertullian than Eusebius, not wistful but forward-looking and missionary, taking the political realm with profound seriousness, but never making it absolute. For a political theology must stay resolutely in the public realm and must engage with the ideologies, structures and practices which are to be found there.

In a post-Christendom era, theology may evacuate the public realm and retreat into the private sphere. This temptation may only be resisted by a theology which realizes that Christian faith, precisely because it is concerned with seeking the Kingdom of God and his righteousness, precisely because it is confession of a particular and universal Lord, cannot avoid relating to the omnipresent civil religions and the political processes which shape women and men so profoundly, for good or ill. Nor may Christian theology allow itself to be absorbed into the public realm, assimilating its values and proclaiming them to be the values of the Kingdom – what Lesslie Newbigin speaks of as 'the Constantinian trap' (Newbigin, 1983, p. 37). 'A good political theology', writes André Dumas, 'does not consist either in watering down the Gospel or in idealizing politics. Each needs to help the other to incarnate the Gospel, rather than reducing it to an impotent idealism, and to demystify politics, rather than making it into a false gospel' (Dumas, 1978, p. 20). There must be a constant recognition of the inter-dependence and interpenetration of the public and private spheres. They depend on one another, and either is impoverished if the other is neglected.

CHAPTER 3

The Promise of Liberation Theology

POLITICAL THEOLOGY AND LIBERATION THEOLOGY

We saw in chapter 1 how in the ancient world political theology was rooted in the various forms of political religion which served to legitimate and interpret the power structure, providing sanctions of a supernatural sort for the maintenance of order and inculcating obedience and reverence for the authorities. The Stoic philosopher Varro distinguished three kinds of theology; fabulous or mythical, natural or philosophical, and political. The mythical and political theologies were mutually supportive, but philosophical theology was to be kept from the ears of the common people as disturbing and unsupportive of traditional allegiances. It is strange, argues Augustine, that the two kinds of theology that make no serious claim to truth are regarded as politically indispensable while the philosophical theology that feels after a truth which is not bounded by the city walls or expressed in a set of childish fables is regarded as inherently seditious. These theologies are palpably devices, inventions for social control, which must be rejected out of hand by any serious seeker after truth, while philosophical theology is in little better case because it has at its heart a fundamental confusion of nature and nature's God, failing to distinguish the creature from the creator. This shows it also to be no more than a human invention which panders to human pride (Augustine, 1945 edn, I, pp. 184–92).

But, in rejecting the theology of the classical world, it is by no means clear that Augustine is rejecting political theology as such; indeed, his own endeavour in *The City of God* could be said to mark the inauguration of a new political theology which relates to the political order in a much more complex and critical way than ancient or classical political theologies were capable of doing, precisely because it sees its task not as sustaining the state but as speaking truth to power, and interpreting what is happening in the light of the Gospel. It is probable that Augustine would have accepted the view later formulated by Peterson that the Christian faith makes the old kind of political theology impossible, because the trinitarian God provides no simple analogical justification for earthly power, because the cross puts in the heart of God suffering powerlessness and because Christian eschatology forbids any identification of earthly peace and earthly kingdoms with the peace of God and the City that is to come (Peterson, 1935; cf. Ruggieri, 1985). But a new, different and distinctively Christian political theology may well be possible. Moltmann, for instance, produces a trinitarian critique of 'political monotheism', 'clerical monotheism' and all political religions which at least implies the possibility of a negative political theology (Moltmann, 1974b, pp. 9–47; 1981, pp. 191–201).

It seems inevitable that Christian theology should relate in some way or other to the political order, if only by default, that is, leaving the status quo intact and unscrutinized. But the use of the term 'political theology' in a Christian context has until recently been highly suspect because it has been associated with what we have labelled 'Eusebian' theology, closely modelled on the old pagan political theologies, and performing the same social function. This impression was reinforced in 1922 by the publication of a book called *Politische Theologie* by Carl Schmitt, who taught that there was a necessary link between theological ideas and political authority even in a secular age. Schmitt advocated a strongly nationalist Catholicism and a reverence for the established order of things. Political disputes were at root theological arguments, and he suggested that theology is inherently conservative.

The more recent use of the term 'political theology', however, dates only from the 1960s, when J. B. Metz, Jürgen Moltmann and the early theologians of liberation 'cleared a new theological space' (Fierro, 1977, p. 17) and freely called their activity in this space political theology, fully aware of the ambiguous past of the term, but confident that the new political theology was not Eusebian and could be defended against the criticisms of people such as Erik Peterson. This new political theology aimed to be practical, public and critical. It was not concerned with conferring an aura of sanctity on politics as much as with questioning and demystifying the political sphere. It is in politics that faith must be expressed today, it was argued, and accordingly theology must be reflection on political praxis.

Christianity, like all religion, preserves a tradition, but for the new political theologians the heart of this tradition is the 'subversive memory' of Jesus which challenges all established order and disturbs complacency. Political theologians have repeatedly been accused of replacing an unholy amalgam of Christian faith and the politics of the Right with a no less acceptable confusion between Christian commitment and commitment to the causes of the Left. Whatever justice there may be in this charge – and there undoubtedly is some – in principle at least the political theologians intend to resist the reduction of faith to the terms of a particular political ideology, while affirming a close and necessary relationship between faith and politics and the need to interpret theology in its social and political context.

Chapter 2 dealt with themes such as secularization which have for some time been central to Western theology, but which do not figure nearly so prominently on the Third World agenda. In Africa, Asia and Latin America religious notions are at least as powerful as secular ideologies in the political arena. Theologies of secularization, such as those of Gogarten, Harvey Cox or van Leeuwen, are singularly unhelpful in the interpretation of what is happening today in Brazil or South Africa. Likewise, the theory that religion belongs in the realm of private life has not had the effect outside the West that it has had in Europe or North America, and the theologies encouraging detachment from the public realm are not generally attractive. Pluralism in the West is usually understood as a concomitant of secularization; it is *secular* pluralism, which is worlds apart from the pluralism appropriate in a pervasively religious society such as India. And while politicization in the West can often be interpreted as a desperate bid for relevance on the part of declining and timid churches, in the Third World the links between the pastoral and the political are so obvious that the political dimension of the Gospel hardly needs defence.

Such questions are high on the agenda of Western theology because it is concerned with how to relate to modernity. But Western modernity is a particular and not a universal phenomenon, shaped by the Enlightenment and the development of industrial capitalism. Thus, the agenda of Western political theology is composed of issues arising from the Enlightenment and from processes and social forces which have shown themselves particularly vigorous in the West in the past century and a half, while liberation theology in Latin America and elsewhere in the Third World is concerned with, and stimulated by, the poverty, oppression, exploitation and social conflicts which, as we shall see in more detail later, dominate the situation and cry out for attention. It is, of course, true that the non-Western world has been deeply influenced by the same forces that have shaped Western modernity. But these forces affect non-Western societies in a different way and are responded to in a fashion which is deeply influenced by cultural factors.

Both Western political theology and liberation theology see the need to relate theory and practice more closely and explicitly than has been common in most modern academic theology. Theology is not done in detachment, but in commitment. It is not a form of pure, objective theory. In engagement, we come to know the truth; and without engagement theology degenerates into abstract, free-ranging speculation. Christian faith, it is held, necessarily involves political commitment, so that Davis can remark that political theology 'is faith as articulated or brought to expression in and through political practice' (Davis, 1980, p. 3), and Moltmann can say that 'the new criterion of theology and of faith is to be found in praxis' (quoted in Kee, 1974, p. 54). But in Western political theology practice is often seen as derived from theory, and lacking a dignity of its own.

Theology may be understood as driving people to practice. But, the theology itself, even if stimulated by contemporary social and political questions, remains general, apparently independent of its context, and ahistorical. In short, in much Western political theology a sharp disjunction remains between theory and practice; the theologian arbitrates and pronounces on practice from a magisterial stance; critical distance must be maintained. Miguez Bonino challenges Moltmann to give concrete content to the 'identification with the oppressed' which Moltmann sees as the implication of faith in the crucified God:

> The poor, the oppressed, the humiliated *are a class* and *live in countries* . . . Are we really for the poor and the oppressed if we fail to see them as a class, as members of oppressed societies? If we fail to say *how*, are we 'for them' in their concrete historical situation? Can we claim a solidarity which has nothing to say about the actual historical forms in which their struggle to overcome oppression is carried forward? . . . Is it possible to claim a solidarity with the poor and to hover above right and left as if the choice did not have anything to do with the matter?
>
> (Bonino, 1975, p. 148)

There is, Bonino claims, no such thing as innocent detachment; even the most abstract theological reasoning has an ideological function. The way to avoid the reduction of the Gospel to a political programme, Miguez Bonino suggests, is not to take refuge in critical detachment, but to illuminate what is going on with the help of the best economics and political science available. In a vigorous and incisive *Open Letter to José Miguez Bonino*, Moltmann rejects the substantive charges, warns against a narrow provincialism in theology and suggests that liberation theology, where it is not derived from European theology, encounters problems and inadequacies of its own. But he does not respond very convincingly to the charges that Western political theology lacks rigorous social analysis and is stronger on the rhetoric than the actuality of solidarity with the oppressed (in Anderson and Stransky, 1979, pp. 57–70).

In a fascinating and aggressive article, Joseph Comblin, a Belgian theologian working in Chile, suggests the paradigm of liberation theology as a humble kind of servant theology, and presses home the attack on Western theology. It is interesting that the most vigorous assault on academic theology should come from one trained in the theological schools of the West, and then exposed to the Latin American situation. His equipment, he suggests, did not stand up to the test of use in this context. In this article he is intent on settling accounts, and, despite exaggerations, there is illumination in what he says. The older, triumphalistic theology which feels that it is self-justifying, that it is a kind of superscience 'safe and secure from the vicissitudes of the world', that it shares in a special way in the holiness and truth of its subject matter, will no longer do, and should never have been accepted, Comblin argues. We are now learning that theology 'is only a human discourse after all' and that theologians are just people who have learned to wield and handle, for whatever purpose, certain words about God. Theologians belong in society, and usually form part of, or are closely related to, the power elite. They have their interests which affect the way they approach theology, and the social position profoundly affects what they can see and the way they see it. 'All theology', he writes, 'is a form of wealth, signifying involvement in the world of the wealthy and solidarity with it' (In Gibellini, 1980, p. 65). Typically, theological systems are stripped of temporal reference and claim universality; they make general claims but cannot generate specific challenges. He instances Christology:

> Academic Christology, which is studied by the experts and enshrined in their manuals and treatises, is frozen in formulas whose meaning is now lost to us. They are reiterated faithfully with little danger of distortion because now they are no more than mere formulas. Our official Christology is a frozen crystal. At the same time our devotion has turned Jesus into an object of cultic devotion. This process of turning the Son of God into an icon projects an intensely religious sense onto him, turning him into a means for satisfying certain religious needs and necessities. But it also deprives him of the possibility of being a revelation and a real teaching.
>
> (in Gibellini, 1980, p. 72)

The kind of theology that we need, and the kind that liberation theology supplies, argues Comblin, is not at the service of the clergy or of the magisterium, but at the service of the Church (meaning the people of God rather than a juridical institution), and through the Church at the service of the world. Academics have expropriated theology from those to whom this 'wealth' properly belongs; a true theology is 'a methodology to restore the use of speech and God's Word to the people of God (in Gibellini, 1980, p. 63). A kind of 'people's theology' is necessary to liberate the Church from false theologies, and restore to the people what is properly theirs.

Thus Comblin is convinced that a central problem of academic theology is that it is distanced from the real life of the grass-roots church, and from the problems of the world as well. The decline of the Western churches provides part of the explanation for the moribundity of academic theology: 'No theology makes sense in a church where nothing is going on. Its whole purpose is to tell us what is happening' (in Gibellini, 1980, p. 68). Christian theology must let the poor speak their piece; it must not speak in their name, on their behalf. In a sense it becomes an anti-theology, or at least it has the negative but vital role of liberating the Church from false theologies and putting in their place not some grandiose systematic construction but a provisional and fragmentary theology designed for a specific situation. This theology, precisely because it is unpretentious, and involves giving back to the people the theological 'wealth' which has been expropriated from them, is praised by its defenders and denounced by its critics as being 'poor theology' – theology at the service of the poor and making no claims to being more than the articulation of how ordinary believers live and understand the faith. Liberation theology arises out of a new praxis, as the poor seek the transformation of their world, a project intimately related both to the Gospel and to the Church. Theology is the servant, the enabler, of the liberating praxis of the Church of the poor.

THE CENTRAL ISSUE FOR LIBERATION THEOLOGY

The central issue for liberation theology, as contrasted with the main concerns of contemporary Western theology, is described thus by Gustavo Gutierrez:

> A goodly part of contemporary theology seems to take its start from the challenge posed by the *nonbeliever*. The nonbeliever calls into question our *religious world*, demanding its through-going purification and revitalization. Bonhoeffer accepted that challenge and incisively formulated the question that underlies much contemporary theological effort: How are we to proclaim God in a world come of age? In a continent like Latin America, however, the main challenge does not come from the nonbeliever but from the *nonhuman* – i.e. the human being who is not recognized as such by the prevailing social order. These are the poor and exploited people, the ones who are systematically and legally despoiled of their being human, those who scarcely know what a human being might be. These nonhumans do not call into question our religious world so much as they call into question our *economic, social, political and cultural world*. Their challenge impels us toward a revolutionary transformation of the very bases of what is now a dehumanizing society. The question, then, is no longer how we are to speak of God in a world come of age; it is rather how to proclaim him Father in a world that is not human and what the implications might be of telling nonhumans that they are children of God.
>
> (in Gibellini, 1980, p. x)

The challenge of the poor and the exploited is not first of all a challenge to theology. It is rather a challenge to Christians and to the Church to show – not just to say – whose side they are on. The response must be practical, it means acts of solidarity, which involve opposition to the economic, social, political and cultural forces of dehumanization as well as the religious legitimations of these forces. Charity, almsgiving, development are inadequate because they do not engage with the causes of human degradation; the praxis of liberation, solidarity with the oppressed, involves confronting the structures of oppression.

In the book which first brought liberation theology to the notice of the Western theological world, Gustavo Gutierrez writes:

> All the political theologies, the theologies of hope, of revolution and of liberation, are not worth one act of genuine solidarity with exploited social classes. They are not worth one act of faith, love, and hope committed – in one way or another – in active participation to liberate man from everything that dehumanizes him and prevents him from living according to the will of the Father.
>
> (Gutierrez, 1974, p. 308)

One cannot, of course, be in solidarity with an abstract, general notion of poor people. People are poor in particular contexts. The poor are members of a social class within a class system. They are the people at the foot of the pile, the victims, the exploited ones. One can only be in solidarity with them where they are and as they are; it is impossible to be alongside some abstract, idealized poor person isolated from context. Solidarity involves a commitment to transforming the situation, to challenging the structures of dehumanization. And this in turn involves endeavouring to understand the forces at work, with the aid of rigorous social analysis. Thus, solidarity implies the need for critical reflection on the situation. The praxis of liberation involves us in turning to social science and theology together to help us to interpret what God is doing in our time, and this disciplined reflection in its turn criticizes our practice. For Gutierrez and most of the liberation theologians there are not two histories – salvation history in which God's hand may be clearly seen and 'ordinary history' which is largely bereft of meaning – but one history, our history, which is the sphere in which salvation and liberation are realized. They are very uneasy about the kind of dualism which we saw most clearly expressed in Luther, and tend to draw the two cities for closer together than Augustine would have accepted.

Liberation theology responds to the challenge of the poor and the oppressed first, by standing with them in solidarity, by a practical commitment; secondly, by seeking to interpret their situation with the help of social analysis; and finally, by sustained theological reflection on what is happening in the light of the tradition.

THE CONTEXT OF LIBERATION THEOLOGY

Liberation theologians argue that all theology is deeply influenced by its context. One cannot properly understand a theological position they claim, without knowing something of the class and economic interests of the theologian, and the broader cultural and socioeconomic situation in which the theologian is working. It has been common for theologians to attend to two aspects of the context, and two alone – to engage in discussion with the influential philosophies of the day, and to see the theological task as in some sense a service of the Church. But even with such nods in the direction of contextuality, most theology has claimed some kind of universality, has seen itself as rising above the particularities of its context to propound truths which are valid everywhere and always, leaving to preaching the application of these timeless truths to any particular situation. Liberation theologians are extremely critical of such pretensions. Those who believe they are transcending their context are, they argue, allowing their interests and their social and cultural context to play an insidious because invisible role in their theological work. And liberation theologians suggest that an atemporal, non-historical theology must have severe difficulty in accommodating itself to the particularity which lies at the heart of Christian faith – that in a specific country, at the particular historical moment, God revealed himself in the man Jesus.

Context cannot be brushed aside; but theology must not become simply a reflection of its context. The liberation theologians believe that theologians must be sensitive in a new way to the context in which they work, recognizing that this context provides resources and a problematic for theology. The social context of theology is seen as a class conflict rather than a harmonious social equilibrium; there are therefore crucial choices to be made in relating to the context, above all the question – whose side are you on? Accordingly, theology, whether it likes it or not, interacts with its context and becomes involved with the conflicts and tensions. A responsible theology, which is determined not simply to be sucked into endorsing the views of one of the conflicting groups, must strive to be sensitive to its context, aware that the context is dynamic and conflictual, and that the role of theology in relation to its social context is to share in transforming it rather that passively accepting it.

Liberation theology initially arose in Latin America, and in examining the soil in which it is rooted, the context in which it arose, we should turn first to history, aware that in speaking in general terms of the history of Latin America we are neglecting the specific histories of different nations, and that to understand a particular theologian coming, say, from Mexico or Colombia, the general history needs to be supplemented by an account of the theologian's immediate context. Keeping that proviso in mind, one may affirm that the history of modern Latin America has been a story of extraordinary oppression and exploitation.

The Conquistadors came as a rapacious aggressors, fully supported by the Church, and with remarkable rapidity took over the major part of the continent, destroying great civilizations and eleminating with savagery any groups who resisted them. The Church for the most part devoted its energies to mass conversions, often at the point of the sword, and to expunging every trace of the old religions of the people. Juan de Zumarraga, the first Bishop of Mexico, boasted in 1531 that he had destroyed more than 500 temples and had smashed some 20,000 idols (Johnson, 1976, p. 402). Indians and Indian converts were treated virtually as an inferior species, an attitude sometimes justified by reference to Aristotle's argument that some people are by nature slaves, fit only to be used as tools by others. The Church authorities, as well as the civil powers, were vehemently opposed to the indigenous cultures and endeavoured to expunge the native languages. A relentless and appallingly successful policy of cultural and religious imperialism was to make Spanish or Portuguese government and economic exploitation rest upon the ideological support of a Church to which everyone belonged and a culture which was unambiguously Hispanic.

As time went on, Indians embraced the Church with enthusiasm and developed the Christianized folk religion which is still so powerful today. But they were kept in strict tutelage and denied education. Few Indians were ordained and none found preferment within the Church. Synods repeatedly declared that natives were not to be ordained or admitted to the religious orders, which were such a potent agency of Spanish power, except as servants. The indigenous peoples were treated at best as infants who could never grow up, at worst as beings barely human. It is hardly surprising that Latin America produced for centuries no innovative or interesting theological ideas, as Paul Johnson explains:

> This huge continent, where paganism was quickly expunged, where great cities, universities and sub-cultures were soon established, where Christianity was united and monopolistic, carefully protected by the State from any hint of heresy, schism or rival, and where the clergy were innumerable, rich and privileged, made virtually no distinctive contribution to the Christian message and insight in over four centuries. Latin America exuded a long, conformist silence.
>
> (Johnson, 1976, p. 407)

The system whereby the Church was the principal agency of social and political control worked well until the eighteenth century, when monarchs in Spain influenced by the Enlightenment began introducing reforms and attempted to distance an 'enlightened' government from a Church deemed obscurantist. Moves by government against the powerful religious orders, particulary the Jesuits, who were suppressed in 1769, were profoundly unpopular among ordinary people, as was the decree of 1812 abolishing 'benefit of clergy', the right of the clergy and the religious to be tried in Church courts and exempted from the ordinary civil law. Clergy provided most of the leadership in a series of revolts leading up to the independence movement in the early nineteenth century, and the masses of the people were solidly behind them. Priests, already becoming well accustomed to exercising a political as well as a religious role, now led their people against the government. When the liberals gained control of Spanish politics in 1820, all but two of the Mexican bishops declared for independence. Faced with a choice between loyalty to a reforming imperial power and a conservative Church which had won their hearts, most people sided with the Church. And with the coming of independence, we find in all the countries of Latin America that the Church was by far the most powerful social institution, claiming the allegiance of the great body of the people, and well accustomed to exerting or influencing political power.

Independence from Spain was far from being the end of dependency for Latin America. Indeed, no sooner was the political control of Spain withdrawn than the countries of Latin America were drawn into the expanding capitalist market economy and quickly became economically dependent on Britain or the United States. Latin America was an outlet for the manufactured goods of the Western industrialized nations, and in return produced beef, bananas, coffee and other agricultural products. With economic dependency went a new and more subtle kind of political control. 'Banana republics' were in effect at the mercy of big North American companies, and at a time of crisis the companies could always fall back on the support of the US government. Many Latin American countries were notoriously unstable politically, and governments with an insecure grip on power are hardly in position to discipline powerful outside economic interests. Nor were weak governments capable of responding effectively to massive poverty and the resultant social unrest, which reinforced instability.

A common response in the 1960s and 1970s was the development of the 'National Security State'. This was an ideology and a type of right-wing military regime which dominated Chile, Brazil and Argentina and was influential elsewhere as well. It stressed the superiority of Western and Christian civilization, particularly as compared with the 'eastern' alternative, represented in the region by Castro's Cuba. But it believed that Western culture required renewal, for it had been perverted by Marx, Freud and other radicals. Economically, the National Security regimes looked to the Chicago School of neoconservative economists for guidance, and sought to run their economies according to the theories of Friedrich von Hayek and Milton Friedman, who advocate the free market as both the surest way to economic prosperity and the only safeguard against the totalitarian socialism that would destroy individual freedom.

Such ideas were, for obvious reasons, attractive to dictators like President Pinochet of Chile, who attempted to administer a

Hayek–Friedman style 'short, sharp shock' to the Chilean economy and society, with a massive bonfire of government economic controls, a sustained attack on trade unions and an attempt to reduce wages to make the Chilean economy more competitive. To say that the experiment did not work is an understatement. Unemployment was massively increased, poverty reached epidemic proportions in the cities and massive social unrest resulted. As a consequence, the government became ever more draconian in its activities, and the promised day when democracy might be restored receded over the horizon.

Like other National Security regimes, Pinochet's junta aims in theory at a restoration of democracy after a period of perhaps painful cultural, economic and political purification. But in reality any return to democracy except one forced upon the regime by popular pressure, as in Argentina, seems less and less likely. And the amount of human suffering involved makes it hard for even the more conservatively inclined bishops to give support to a government which sees its primary task as the preservation of Christian civilization against communism. In the congregations in the shanty towns and in the countryside, where people's daily experience is of poverty and oppression, it is not surprising that the longing is for liberation. As Gustavo Gutierrez has pointed out: 'Latin American misery and injustice go too deep to be responsive to palliatives. Hence we speak of social revolution, not reform; of liberation, not development; of socialism, not modernization of the prevailing system' (Gutierrez, 1983, p. 45).

TWO EXEMPLARS OF LIBERATION

This very sketchy outline of the history of Latin America provides more than an indication of the historical context in which liberation theology grew; it also points to an alternative heritage with which liberation theologians identify. Certain moments and figures in that history suggest possibilities and responses which are of particular relevance to the way the liberation theologians understand their task. Some mention must be made of two figures, in particular, whose example has been especially relevant among liberation theologians, one – Bartolome de Las Casas – from early Spanish days, and another – Camilo Torres – from recent times. The Latin American Church, argues Sobrino, is rediscovering its historical identity by re-reading its history from the standpoint of the poor and, in the process, rediscovering the significance of those who in their day made the Church a church of the poor (Sobrino, 1985, p. 112).

Bartolome de Las Casas arrived in South America in 1502 and was quickly outraged by the treatment to which he saw the Indians subjected. He devoted most of his life to their cause, arguing against the prominent theologian J. G. de Sepulveda that Indians were fully human and were not the natural slaves spoken of by Aristotle. They were entitled to freedom, and to be treated as human beings on a level with the Spaniards. He protested vehemently against the oppression and maltreatment of the Indians and managed for a few years to secure legislation for their proper protection. But, by the end of his life, his endeavours appeared to have met total failure (Hanke, 1959; Witvliet, 1985, pp. 11–12). Gutierrez sees Las Casas as affirming that salvation is bound up with the achievement of social justice; the two are not identical, but they must not be separated. The Spaniards, he taught, by their degradation and exploitation of the Indians, had put their own salvation in jeopardy, 'for it is impossible for anyone to be saved who does not observe justice'. Judgement, he believed, began in the household of faith, and the salvation of the heathen Indians was less in doubt than that of the Spaniards who despoiled them. Accordingly, Las Casas saw the Indians more as God's poor, those for whom God has a special care, than as 'heathens' to be converted, by force if necessary. Once again, he had to oppose Sepulveda, who taught that the subjection of the Indians to the Spaniards was right and proper, and was indeed for their own good. Sepulveda was willing to justify wars to establish this subjection, which he saw as natural, and also the necessary condition for the evangelization of the natives. Sepulveda, says Gutierrez, is the type of theologian common in Latin America and elsewhere, whose theology justifies oppression, just as Las Casas is the type of theologian who sides with the poor. Las Casas attacked Sepulveda for an intellectualized theology abstracted from reality which in effect legitimated the most intolerable practices; he did not not know the Indians or share their sufferings; he did not accept responsibility for the practical consequences of his thought. Las Casas' central insight was that Christ speaks to us from among the Indians. He had seen 'Jesus Christ, our God, scourged and afflicted and crucified, not once, but thousands of times'. Las Casas and others like him were well versed in traditional academic theology, and perfectly capable of deploying their arguments in a strictly intellectual way. And yet they broke new paths in theology, once they had read the Gospel from the viewpoint of the 'scourged Christs of the Indies' (Gutierrez, 1983, pp. 194–7).

In more recent times, the figure of Camilo Torres (1929–66), the Colombian priest who died as a guerrilla, had a profound and challenging impact on the development of liberation theology. From a privileged family, Torres understood his call to the priesthood as a way of giving himself without reserve to the love of his neighbours. After studies in theology and sociology at Louvain, he was appointed chaplain to the National University. There he began a serious analysis of the national situation and taught students that the greatest need was for Christians to love people in their concrete situations. Love, he argued, involves intelligent efforts to challenge and change the structures of lovelessness, so that the hungry can be fed and the needy cared for. Both love and the priestly vocation therefore prescribe revolution. Torres was inhibited from speaking further on social issues by his ecclesiastical superiors, and laicized. However, he continued to regard himself as a priest. 'The Catholic who is not a revolutionary is living in mortal sin', he proclaimed (Gerassi, 1973, p. 9). He believed that in a society as deeply implicated in injustice and lovelessness as Colombia, it was impossible for the Church to be the Church, or for the eucharist, the sacrament of unity and justice, to be properly celebrated. 'I took off my cassock to be more fully a priest', he declared (Gerassi, 1973, p. 9). He explained his revolutionary priestly vocation in a statement which deserves to be quoted at length:

When circumstances prevent men from actively consecrating their lives to Christ, it is the priest's duty to combat these circumstances even if he must forfeit the right to officiate at Eucharistic rites, which have meaning only if Christians are so consecrated.

Within the present structure of the church, it has become impossible for me to continue acting as priest in the external aspects of our religion. However, the Christian priesthood consists not only of officiating at external ritual observances. The Mass, which is at the centre of the priesthood, is fundamentally communal. But the Christian community cannot worship in an authentic way unless it has first effectively put into practice the precept of love for fellow man. I chose Christianity because I believed that in it I would find the purest way to serve my fellow man. I was chosen by Christ to be a priest forever because of the desire to consecrate my full time to the love of my fellow man.

As a sociologist, I have wanted this love to be translated into efficient service through technology and science. My analysis of Colombian society made me recognize that revolution is necessary to feed the hungry, give drink to the thirsty, clothe the naked, and procure a life of well-being for the needy majority of our people. I believe that the revolutionary struggle is appropriate for the Christian and the priest. Only by revolution, by changing the concrete conditions of our country, can we enable men to practise love for each other.

Throughout my ministry as a priest, I have tried in every way possible to persuade the laymen, Catholic or not, to join the revolutionary struggle. In the absence of a massive response, I have resolved to join the revolution myself, thus carrying out part of my work of teaching men to love God by loving each other. I consider this action essential as a Christian, as a priest, and as a Colombian. But such action, at this time, is contrary to the discipline of the present church. I do not want to break the discipline of the Church, but I also do not want to betray my conscience.

Therefore, I have asked his Eminence the Cardinal to free me from my obligations as a member of the clergy, so that I may serve the people on a temporal level. I forfeit one of the privileges I deeply love – the right to officiate as priest at the external rites of the Church. But I do so to create the conditions that will make these rites more authentic.

I believe that my commitment to live a useful life, efficiently fulfilling the precept of love for my fellow man, demands this sacrifice of me. The highest standard by which human decisions must be measured is the all-surpassing love that is true charity, I accept all the risks that this standard demands of me.

(Gerassi, 1973, pp. 334–5)

On 15 February 1966, Father Camilo Torres was ambushed and killed by the military. His death, even more than his life, was a powerful challenge to a Church hierarchy tempted to collude with oppression, and a stimulus to the development of liberation theology as reflection upon loving, liberative, world-transforming praxis.

THE RADICALIZING OF THE LATIN AMERICAN CHURCHES

Latin America is a Christian continent. Some 80 per cent of the population are Roman Catholic, and most of the rest belong to mainstream or pentecostalist Protestant groups. This means that in the most obvious sociological sense the Church is the church of the people. And when one reflects that in Latin America the majority of the people are poor, it becomes clear that we are dealing with a church of the poor. It is, of course, true that a church which numerically is predominantly composed of poor people may nevertheless be led by a hierarchy which is middle class and does not see its role as in any way representing the interests of the poor, or acting as a mouthpiece for them. Such a church may act as an effective agency of ideological and social control. But in many countries of Latin America in the 1960s and 1970s the cries of anguish from the increasing misery of the urban slums and the gigantic concentrations of squalor that sprang up around rapidly growing cities such as São Paulo were heard by increasing numbers of bishops, who in response gradually moved to a more radical position. Priests attempting to exercise a pastoral ministry among people in an inherently brutalizing situation demanded that their pastors and the Church as an institution should listen to them and to how they were understanding the Gospel, and take a stand on the side of the poor by calling for justice and a decent social order. Priests felt impotent, 'prisoners', in an ecclesiastical system and a style of priestly life which set them apart from their people, and made it hard for them to share the life or the agonies of their flocks. They asked for liberation from 'the pastoral machine' and a throughgoing reform of the Church in order to be able to serve and energize the people better (Gheerbrant, 1974, pp. 123–39). This kind of *cri de coeur* had a cumulative impact; both bishops and theologians responded, and began to see their role in a very different light.

The new radicalism of the Latin American churches was, of course, strongly resisted by many traditionalist bishops, and the political authorities, initially disconcerted by finding that the Church had become subversive, did what they could to contain and control the movement. Rome meanwhile vaccilated. There is no doubt that the Second Vatican Council had released forces of renewal at every level which contributed powerfully to the upsurge of life in the Latin American churches. But from time to time the Vatican took fright at what was happening, and attempted to apply the brakes.

A crucial event was the General Conference of the Latin American Hierarchies held at Medellin in Colombia in 1968 which was attended by Pope Paul VI. The conservatives believed that the Pope would rebuke and restrain the radicals; the radicals hoped that the Pope would act as their mouthpiece in addressing the power elite. In the event, the radicals triumphed. The conference became 'the springboard for the Latin American theology of liberation' (Fierro, 1977 p. 13), because, as Guiterrez claimed, 'At Medellin the Latin American Church . . . realistically perceived the world in which it was and clearly saw its place in that world' (Gutierrez, 1974, p. 134). The Conference's statement on peace and justice called on the whole Church, and particularly the bishops, to defend the rights of the poor and the oppressed, to speak out against abuses, to encourage the people to form their own grass-roots organizations, to urge the developed countries to pay a just price for raw materials from the Third World and to denounce 'the unjust attempts by powerful nations to prevent weaker nations from achieving self-determination' (Gheerbrant, 1974, p. 257). This momentous event was followed a decade later by the General

Conference of the Latin American Hierarchies held at Pueblo in 1979, which clearly declared a preferential option for the poor, and gave further encouragement to the base communities – the 'grass-roots church' – and to the development of liberation theology. These two conferences gave a major impetus to the development of liberation theology which now saw itself as having the encouragement of the hierarchies and even of the Pope himself.

A NEW WAY OF DOING THEOLOGY

Traditional academic theology has concentrated increasingly on developing sophisticated ways of understanding the past, of interpreting biblical documents to find out their original meaning and of relating the formulations of faith in the ancient world to their original context. In order to fulfil this task, it has had to seek the help of other disciplines, the most relevant of which have been philology, philosophy and history. Far less attention has been given to today's world, to how to understand and proclaim the Gospel today, to analysing the opportunities and problems for Christian faith in the modern world, and indeed to asking what God is doing in our times. Liberation theology believes that the tasks of opening up the past and of opening up the present must be held together, that the past and the present must be enabled to interrogate one another. But in order to allow this to take place we need tools to help us understand the present which may differ from the tools which help us understand the past. In short, a theology which seeks to construe the present must use the sciences which deal with the present, particularly the social sciences, just as the study of Christian origins would be impossible without the tools of biblical criticism, classical philology, archaeology, etc. Because liberation theology is concerned with this kind of dialogue and questioning between past and present, it must in addition to the disciplines that are the traditional partners of theology turn to the best forms of social analysis and social philosophy that are available – and that means those that provide the greatest illumination of what is going on.

For liberation theologians, Marxism is the necessary dialogue partner. This is because Marxism provides a compelling analysis of exploitation and oppression, of social division and injustice, and carries with the analysis suggestions as to the appropriate response to such a situation. Most other available options are bland about social conflict or can hardly see it because they are so obsessed with equilibrium, harmony and social cohesion. Marxism faces the realities of class conflict and opposing interests in a way which seems faithful to what people involved with the poor in Latin America have encountered 'on the ground', and sees these conflicts as playing a positive role in movement towards a more just social order.

When it is pointed out that Marxism is an avowedly atheistic system, liberation theologians reply that Christian theology has done business before with atheistic or unchristian philosophies. The situation today *vis-à-vis* Marxism, they say, is not much different from the theological crisis in the thirteenth century, when Aristotle was reintroduced into Western Europe. The problem then, as now, was that a body of thought which was on its own account clearly non-Christian impressed many people as substantially true and as a significant guide to the investigation of reality. Two ways of dealing with such a situation are possible; either one asserts that there are *two* truths, valid in different realms so that the incompatibilities seem unimportant because the two truths do not really interact with one another; or an attempt is made to reconcile the two truths, on the assumption that two contradictory statements cannot both be true and that our apprehension of reality may be enriched by bringing the two bodies of truth into dialogue with one another. St Thomas Aquinas's aim was the reconciliation of Aristotle and the Christian tradition to form a new synthesis. And Christian theology has always engaged with and used the dominant philosophies of the age. The danger of a distorting syncretism is always pressed, but few theologians can claim to be doing a *pure* theology, innocent of any involvement with non-theological ideas. If such a theology were possible it would probably be largely unintelligible because it would be nothing more than a reiteration or incantation of sentences from the Bible or from the Fathers – which are themselves, of course, expressed in terms of the thought-forms of their day. Even Protestant theology at its most 'biblical' and scornful of the seductions of philosophy in fact has recourse to the conceptional structures of its culture and betrays influences which are not strictly theological.

Surreptitious and unacknowledged influence is probably more dangerous than the open dialogue, entered into fully conscious both of the dangers and the opportunities involved, which characterizes liberation theology's encounter with Marxism. Liberation theologians opted for Marxism because Marxist analysis, they believe, provides the most convincing account of what it happening in their societies. In struggling for justice, they have again and again found themselves shoulder to shoulder with Marxists and been surprised to find how much they have in common and how much they can learn from one another. They in general carefully distinguish 'Marxism as a worldview' from 'Marxism as a tool for understanding social conflict and social change'. Thus they attempt to use the tools without buying the toolbag. Yet, liberation theologians are not ignorant of other contemporary social philosophies. Many of them, such as Miguez Bonino or Juan Segundo know their way about the debates associated with names like Rawls, and Nozick, Friedman, Keynes and von Hayek. It is simply that they do not find these other approaches as convincing or relevant in their situations as a Marxist form of analysis, or they have had experience of their being used to defend tyranny, injustice and oppression.

Liberation theology understands its distinctive way of doing theology as a kind of hermeneutical circle in the course of which questions and suspicions arising from our situation and our commitments are addressed to the tradition, to our practice and to social reality. Thus, the way we construe the world, read the Bible and express our commitments in action are deepened. It is perhaps not as much a circle as a spiral, for one never returns to the same point; progress is made, understanding is enlarged and practice becomes more appropriate. Much academic theology, liberation theologians consider, is 'going round in circles', for the questions it addresses to the data are artificial and unimportant and cannot elicit answers that are existentially relevant, fresh or penetrating. A true hermeneutic circle or spiral, according to Segundo, demands two preconditions. The first is that:

> The questions rising out of the present be rich enough, general enough, and basic enough to force us to change our customary conceptions of life, death, knowledge, society, politics and the world in general. Only a change of this sort, or at the very least a pervasive suspicion about our ideas and value judgements concerning these things, will enable us to reach the theological level and force theology to come back down to reality and ask itself new and decisive questions.
>
> (Segundo, 1977, pp. 8–9).

The second precondition is a willingness to alter received interpretations of Scripture and theological formulations, for without this the new questions will go unanswered, or receive hackneyed, traditional responses.

The liberationists' way of doing theology starts with *engagement*. The issues that really interest them arise out of their stress that the God with whom we are engaged is the living God, active in today's world, who is encountered in particular contexts, and is to be responded to in quite specific ways. God is implicated in history, and it is there, in the world, as well as in Scripture and worship, that we meet him. The abstract, atemporal problem of belief in God has little interest for liberation theologians, because for them the pressing and interesting questions are to do with what faith in God means today, in this specific context. Furthermore, faith in God, as the Bible teaches, involves commitment to the neighbour – the two commitments cannot be separated. And – again following clear biblical teaching – there should be a special care for the needy and the poor neighbour. Thus, faith in God is seen as inseparable from commitment to the poor; and once again not to an abstract, general idea of the poor, or a spiritualized notion of the humble poor, but to the poor as they are around us in our society.

This specific commitment has various important implications. We should expect to learn from the poor of the things of God. And we can only hear them if we are close, alongside, in solidarity. So theology should be done in solidarity with the poor. And that means taking sides. Put in social-scientific categories, it means to recognize that the poor belong to a class, within a class system which is at least in part the cause of their poverty. Theology therefore not only listens to the poor but it asks why they are poor, and what can be done about it. Moreover, engagement demands involvement in the life of the Church. Latin American theologians do not appear to have the same scruples as many Western theologians in regarding theology as a function of the Church, and the theologian as having a responsibility to the Church as well as to the academy. It is not that they are complacent or uncritical of the institutional Church – indeed they have caused more trouble for Cardinal Ratzinger and the traditionalists than all the academic radicals of Europe and America put together – but they cannot conceive a Christian theology which is not also a Church theology. Detachment from the Church is almost as harmful for theology in their view as detachment from the world. A living theology must be engaged with God, with people, especially the poor, with the world, and with the Church.

This emphasis, on *praxis*, is also deeply rooted in the Christian tradition, but has been rather neglected by academic theology, at least until recent times. Faith becomes effective in love (Gal. 5:6), and through loving we come to know God and our neighbour. As the Johannine writings in particular stress, the truth is something to be done, to be lived. In other words, we learn by doing: as Vico pointed out, human beings know well only what they do. And action which changes things, which transforms or converts (to use a more conventional theological term) both us and our context is the best path to knowledge. As Gutierrez puts it:

> Truth, for the contemporary human being, is something *verified*, something 'made true'. Knowledge of reality that leads to no modification of that reality is not verified, does not become true ... The praxis that transforms history is not a moment in the feeble incarnation of a limpid, well-articulated theory, but the matrix of authentic knowledge and the acid test of the validity of that knowledge. It is the place where human beings recreate their world and shape themselves. It is the place where they

know the reality in which they find themselves, and thereby know themselves as well.

(Gutierrez, 1983, p. 59)

Here we have a pragmatic concept of the truth – truth is what works. The praxis of love transforms reality. It is not a matter of torturing nature to make her reveal her secrets, but of eliciting the truth through love.

The emphasis on praxis in liberation theology has led some people to regard it as encouraging an unthinking activism. But praxis includes reflection as well as action and, although liberation theologians tend to affirm the priority of action, this is to be understood as a corrective to an overemphasis on theory in theology. They really believe in the necessity for a dialetic between theory and practice, and have no use for an unreflective practice or for a free-floating theory. Theory needs to be rooted in, and tested by, practice, and practice requires a constantly reassessed sense of direction such as can only be provided by theory. We have here a relationship between theory and practice, knowing and doing, which is defensible in explicitly biblical terms: truth is something to be *done*, not observed or manipulated, and the one 'who does the truth comes to the light' (John 3: 21). Truth is to be loved, not dealt with in a detached way, and the loving is the way to knowing. Thus, liberation theologians see a close relationship between spirituality and their way of doing theology. Loving attention to God necessarily involves loving attention to the poor, for whom God has a special care, and to the inward and outward obstacles to the realization of God's purposes of love. Contemplation becomes a radical and a subversive activity.

To sum up the thrust of the distinctive method of liberation theology: *understanding* results from the suspicions and the questions generated by engagement and praxis. Liberation theologians commonly refer to this as the 'hermeneutics of suspicion'. We are forced to pose new questions, or old questions in a different way, by our experience of commitment in the world. We question ourselves, our behaviour, the way we understand and affect our world and the people around us, and the way we construe the tradition. And we ask a new type of question about social forces and social conflicts, enquiring about the social balance of power, and who benefits and who loses, and what can be done to change things. The role of ideology also has to be examined to see how far it is used as a cloak to disguise what is really happening, how far it is an instrument of social control, helping to keep people 'in their place' and content with oppressive conditions, and how far it illumines reality and shows us what is going on. And received interpretations of the Bible and theological orthodoxies also need to be reassessed: have they perhaps failed to take important pieces of evidence into account? Have they been subtly watered down, so that we can live with them more comfortably? Whose interests do they serve? Engagement and action/contemplation force us back to fundamentals, and make us address new questions to the tradition with real urgency. And thereby our understanding of that tradition is challenged, deepened and transformed.

In this process, 'the hermeneutic spiral', the promise of liberation theology finds its fulfilment, as engagement, action and understanding interact with one another. That promise is of a renewal of theology, a strengthening of authentic commitment, a radical reform of the Church, and a more just and caring social order – all with a view to the coming of the Kingdom.

CHAPTER 4

The Bible and Political Theology

Liberation theology may be said to have sprung from a rediscovery of the Bible, and it argues very strongly for the political relevance of Scripture and for the need for its political interpretation. Although it uses freely the tools of modern critical exegesis, liberation theology carries on a running guerrilla warfare with the present enterprise of Western biblical scholarship. It recapitulates themes, emphases and approaches common in the Church in earlier ages, but adds emphatically modern and novel hermeneutical principles. It assumes, rather than arguing for, a 'high' doctrine of scriptural authority and sees the Bible as the most relevant of books for understanding and motivation in the social conflicts of today.

In their turn, liberation and political theologians are vigorously castigated for being precritical, naive and simplistic in their use of Scripture. They are accused of combining an unbalanced and narrow selectivity in the passages they regard as hermeneutical keys with quite unexamined axioms of the unity and authority of the Bible. Moltmann is said to be a great Christian poet who has strayed into theology; his thought 'moves back and forth between exegesis and poetry . . . but he seldom asks himself whether we today can make the thinking of the Bible our own' (Fierro, 1977, pp. 171, 323). Another charge that is frequently aired is that liberation theologians, like fundamentalists, use texts and passages wrenched from their contexts as weapons in debate, only now the main discussions are political rather than ecclesiastical. For their part, liberation theologians attempt to expose the 'objectivity' of scientific biblical scholarship as spurious; no such detachment from one's interests and position in society is possible and, accordingly, their ideas are being used directly or indirectly to legitimate existing power structures.

Any discussion about how to use the Bible with specific reference to its political implications raises a range of important issues about biblical interpretation. Is there a relation between a proper reading of Scripture and commitment to a specific kind of praxis? Is it proper to look to the Bible to generate and shape political attitudes and behaviour, or is such an expectation fundamentally misconceived? Can one move directly – or at all – from Biblical premises to political conclusions? Does Scripture dictate a tightly-drawn political ethic, or does it merely provide politically relevant illumination in terms of a vision, a story or a horizon rather than answers to specific political quandaries? As we shall see, most of these questions had been shelved in Western theology for some time. The rise of modern political theology has reopened a debate which many people believed had been concluded with general agreement that the relevance of the Bible to today's politics was at best tangential, and that the problems involved in any kind of political reading of Scripture were so serious that it must be virtually ruled out of court. Many scholars see in political theology's use of the Bible the resuscitation of old approaches which had been abandoned long ago as intellectually untenable; yet liberation theologians respond that contemporary academic theology has suffered from a failure of nerve about the relevance of Scripture to the modern world and has become blind to the direct bearing of many passages on today's problems. Older ways of reading, left behind by critical scholarship, might require to be repossessed and adapted to contemporary use because they address more real and pressing issues than those engaged with by the mainstream of academic biblical scholarship.

THE BIBLE AND POLITICAL LIFE: FAILURE OF NERVE?

Liberation theologians have sometimes been accused of being, to all intents and purposes, fundamentalists who use a proof-text approach, finding verses or passages wrenched from their context to support positions often reached quite independently of the Bible, and of failing to appreciate the hermeneutical problems involved in applying Scripture to present-day problems. However, the use of Scripture by fundamentalists is quite different in various ways. In practice, they treat the Bible as a textbook of timeless ethical norms, without diversity or contradiction (apart from those that arise from the fact that certain Old Testament injunctions have been superseded under the new covenant): the effect is legalistic, conservative and often oppressive. Furthermore, it is commonly assumed that the major and almost exclusive interest of Scripture is in individual behaviour rather than social, economic and political structures and collective behaviour. Respect for the text means that account has to be taken of structures such as the state. But the Bible does not represent a challenge to the established order of things as much as a call to individuals to behave ethically within given structures (Catherwood, 1964, 1975, 1979).

Political theologians take issue with fundamentalism's reluctance to take history with full seriousness, with its tendency towards political conservatism, and with its excessive concentration on individual and family ethics. Political theology totally rejects the individualism of fundamentalism, together with its claim that the Bible is a source for atemporal, unhistorical, free-floating truths, doctrines and principles. But political theology shares with fundamentalism two things: a tendency to stress the similarities rather than the differences between the world of the Bible and the world of today, and a conviction that commitment (albeit of a rather different sort) is needed for a proper reading of the text. Both emphasize the unity rather than the diversity of the Bible. Both are suspicious of the pretensions of scientific exegesis, but on very different grounds – fundamentalists suggest that scientific exegesis is corrosive of received certainties, while political theologians see the claim to objectivity as spurious and misleading.

Another line of theologically conservative exegesis which has a major political concern is the attempt to apply biblical prophecies directly to the interpretation of today's events. This 'prophetic approach' has, of course, a long and sometimes bizarre ancestry. Much of it is naive in its conclusions and irresponsible and uncritical in its use of Scripture. The dangers of an apocalyptic interpretation of relations between the United States and the Soviet Union, for example, are only too obvious. A prophetic approach often reduces complex and morally ambiguous situations to black and white terms, encouraging trigger-happy behaviour by inculcating the belief that God is on our side.

A good deal of this 'prophetic' interpretation of the Bible centres today on the attempt to understand the significance of the state of Israel and its relations with its neighbours. Typically, the return of the Jews to the land is seen as a uniquely significant fulfilment of prophecy, as following with some kind of dogmatic necessity upon the resurrection of Jesus, and as an unequivocal expression of the will of God. The Zionist conviction that the Jews have a perpetual divine right to the land is firmly endorsed. Israel's military successes are signs of divine approval. Furthermore, as David Torrance writes, in their dealings with the state of Israel 'the peoples and nations of the world are encountering God and are being judged by God' (Torrance, 1982, p. 11). Since 'Israel and all that concerns her is a light shining in the darkness and a witness before the nations of the world', it is hardly surprising that we read that 'the other nations and the Church cannot rightly stand back from Israel in criticism and judgement of her' (Torrance, 1982, p. 110).

This kind of biblical/political argument appears to imply that the state of Israel is exempt, for mysterious but biblical reasons, from the ordinary norms of political morality, and that its existence and activity transcend the ambiguities and relativities of the political sphere. D. W. Torrance and his brother, T. F. Torrance, see the return to the land and even the relations of Israel and her neighbours as direct fulfilment of Old Testament prophecy and demonstrations of the faithfulness of God; it is axiomatic to their thinking that the land continues to have an unquestioned and indeed enhanced position under the new convenant; and the special stringency of God's judgement on Church and Israel retreats into the wings:

The resistance of the nations to God and his way of salvation is increasingly manifest in their opposition to Israel. Their attitude to Israel is the test of their attitude to God and the test whereby they will be blessed or judged by God. Such scriptures as Zechariah 12 make it clear that God will judge every nation by its attitude to Israel. Nations that compromise over Israel will themselves be compromised; those that seek to break Israel will themselves be broken and nations that go against Israel will be opposed by God. This is again clearly stated by God in Isaiah 60.12, 'that nation and kingdom that will not serve thee shall perish, yea, those nations shall be utterly wasted'. In Jeremiah 30.11, the Lord states the matter even more emphatically, 'for I am with thee, saith the Lord, to save thee: though I will make a full end of all nations whither I have scattered thee, yet I will not make a full end of thee'... The destiny of the Jews and the destiny of the world belong together and the peace and prosperity of Israel under God is essential for the peace and prosperity of the world.

(Torrance, 1982, p. 111)

Such attempts to produce a political theology of Israel are simplistic and ill-conceived exegesis, although the significance of the endeavour should be endorsed. But it is important to recognize that such writers are convinced that the Bible gives clues to the understanding of history, that God is active in the public events of the day, and that the Bible has relevance and significance far beyond the private, domestic and acclesiastical realms. The Bible certainly does provide symbolic resources for the interpretation of 'the signs of the times', but these must be used responsibly and critically.

Another form of politically relevant exegesis was developed in the movement called 'biblical theology' which was influential in the 1940s and 1950s. Here, a rejection of fundamentalism and an emphatic embracing of biblical criticism were combined with a very strong stress on the unity of Scripture and a belief that the norms to be elicited from the Bible are applicable in a relatively unproblematic way to modern conditions, or indeed to the conditions of any age. The Bible is witness to the work in history of the 'God who acts' – to borrow the title of G. Ernest Wright's influential monograph in the SCM Press's *Studies in Biblical*

Theology. Immersion in 'the strange world of the Bible' provides the clues for discerning the signs of the times, for the same God is still active today. It is *the Bible as a whole*, rather than specific texts or passages, which is authoritative and may be regarded as the vessel of the Word of God.

Karl Barth was very much presiding genius of the biblical theology movement. He is quite clear that neither ethical norms nor interpretations of what is going on can be simply extracted in proof-text fashion from the Bible. One must rather regard the Bible as a compendium of God's specific dealings with people; saturation in the Bible helps to make one alert to the concrete and specific Word of God addressed to our present situation. A rather different approach is found in Reinhold Niebuhr, another of the gurus of the biblical theology movement. Niebuhr is no less insistent on the need for Christian ethics and Christian judgements on political issues to be rooted in the Bible, but for him the central hermeneutical key is a productive and irresolvable tension between the 'impossible ethic' of the Cross and the Sermon on the Mount, and the rules which have to guide behaviour in a sinful world. The Cross and the Sermon on the Mount are not irrelevant; they may not be set aside and forgotten in favour of a quite unbiblical prudential ethic; they stand in judgement and promise over the compromises necessary in the world. Barth and Niebuhr are typical of the biblical theology movement in affirming in the most emphatic fashion that Christian ethics must be rooted in the Bible, but that the passage from the Bible to today's decisions is no simple matter. Yet for them the complexity arises not so much because of the passage of time, or the cultural gap between the context of the reading and of the writing, as because of the unconditional and absolute demands and injunctions of the Bible.

Typical products of the biblical theology movement in the field of social ethics were the three *Ecumenical Biblical Studies*; Alan Richardson's *The Biblical Doctrine of Work* (1952), G. Ernest Wright's *The Biblical Doctrine of Man in Society* (1954) and H.-H. Schrey, H. H. Walz and W. A. Whitehouse, *The Biblical Doctrine of Justice and Law* (1955). These books were the result of widespread study preparatory to the Evanston

Assembly of the World Council of Churches. Some general points about such productions deserve brief mention. First, note the definite articles: there was a strong stress on the *unity* of the Bible's teaching, linked with a reluctance to admit significant diversity, a unity which arises from the central motif of 'the ongoing redemptive activity of God in the history of one people, reaching its fulfilment in Jesus Christ' (Schrey et al., 1955, p. 47). Secondly, there was little interest in, or awareness of, the problem of interpreting a text developed in one cultural and historical context so that it might be understood and applied in a very different situation. There was a strong tendency to make absolute 'the biblical worldview' and assume its universal relevance. Thirdly, there was a tendency for biblical exposition to become increasingly a task for the 'experts', who had acquired the tools necessary for a reading which was at the same time objective and spoke from faith to faith. The unintended effect of this was increasingly to locate the serious reading of the Bible in the academy, and to take the responsibilities of biblical interpretation away from the people. Connected with this was the risk that scholarly preoccupations and the social context of an elite of expert expositors would heavily condition the reading of Scripture at the expense of life issues and the needs of the Church. To give one example: the book on justice and law (Schrey et al., 1955) has hardly anything to say about any concrete modern issues of justice. Instead, it engages primarily with abstract philosophical and theological matters. An absolutized biblical theology is set up which claims to relativise all human ideologies and political systems. But, in the process, it seems quite forgotten that the justice of which the Bible speaks has a major bearing on the situation of the poor and the oppressed.

Biblical theology as a coherent and dominant orthodoxy collapsed in the 1960s under onslaughts from James Barr and others. In relation to ethical and political issues, interest now focused on the problems and complexities of moving from the Bible to modern problems. 'There is no direct route from the Bible to particular ethical decisions', writes Ronald Preston: 'What the Bible does is to provide a basic orientation, or stance, or vision of goodness which we bring alongside particular

situations whose empirical nature we have to investigate'
(Preston, 1981, p. 60). But when Preston discusses specific
economic and social issues he does not often turn to the Bible for
illumination. Similarly, G. R. Dunstan concludes an essay on
'Theological method in the deterrence debate' by writing: 'If
appeal be made to the Bible, the Bible must be used with the
utmost exegetical integrity – a condition which excludes the
uncritical extrapolation of words and acts from the historical
context of the mission of Jesus and the experience of Him in the
primitive Apostolic community to the political context of our
own day' (Dunstan, 1982, p. 51). And in the same essay he notes
with approval that 'canonists and moralists have had to go
outside the strictly theological tradition, into those of philosophy and law, in order to work on the world's problems to any
effect at all.' He then suggests that the most important specifically Christian contribution is 'the character which it [the
Gospel] imprints upon Christian men carrying responsibility in
the relevant exercise of judgement and use of power' – and particularly their prudence. It would appear that the Bible has been
left behind in favour of a purely prudential ethic.

   Behind some of this way of thinking lurks the hermeneutical
despair of a book such as D. E. Nineham's *The Use and Abuse of
the Bible* (1976), based on an exaggerated pessimism about the
possibility of communicating from one culture or age to
another. Nineham believes that other cultures and ages are
inaccessible, so that historical understanding becomes not only
hard but virtually impossible. This means that Christians
should be emancipated from their exclusive preoccupation with
biblical authority, and should feel free to look for guidance
wherever it may be found. In even sharper fashion, Jack T.
Sanders suggests we must no longer treat the Bible as authoritative in ethics:

> The ethical positions of the New Testament are the children of
> their own times and places, alien and foreign to this day and age.
> Amidst the ethical dilemmas which confront us, we are now at
> least relieved of the need or temptation to begin with Jesus, or
> the early Church, or the New Testament, if we wish to develop
> coherent ethical positions. We are freed from bondage to that
> tradition, and we are able to propose, with the authority of the

Epistle of James, that tradition and precedent must not be allowed to stand in the way of what is humane and right.

(Sanders, 1976, p. 130)

Such attitudes abandon the endeavour to relate the original meaning of a biblical passage to its meaning today; indeed, this kind of scholarship appears no longer to address itself to the modern meaning and use of the Bible in ethics, and leaves the preacher and the Christian either to look elsewhere than the Bible for the guidance that is required, or perhaps to twist and manipulate the Bible to support conclusions reached on quite other grounds.

There have, of course, been scholarly studies which take a more positive view of the possibilities of using biblical material in ethics and seek a fusion of the two horizons, our own and that of the text, in relation to ethical issues. A fine example of this kind of writing is Thomas W. Ogletree's *The Use of the Bible in Christian Ethics* (1984). Ogletree is convinced that the significance of biblical texts is not confined to the past, to the intentions of the writers or to the context which influenced the writing. Unlike Nineham, he sees important possibilities of communicating from one age to another across vast cultural differences. But only if we take the particularities of the original setting very seriously and attend to the ways in which the passage has been used and interpreted down the ages may we find it useful in handling the concrete and different problems of today. Ogletree and others have demonstrated that a scholarly and responsible use of the Bible in ethics is in principle possible. But recent Western theology has produced few convincing instances of how this might be done in relation to specific issues. And it is precisely at this point that the use of the Bible which underlies liberation theology comes as such a challenge.

THE BIBLE IN THE HANDS OF THE PEOPLE

It is less correct to speak of the recovery of the Bible *in* liberation theology than of the new popular engagement *with* the Bible on which liberation theology is based. It was not liberation theology which directed people's attention to the Bible but the repossession of the Bible by the people of God, so powerfully encouraged in Roman Catholic circles by the Second Vatican Council, which stimulated and shaped liberation theology. The Second Vatican Council represented, it should be noted, a radical reversal of a common attitude of the Roman Catholic Church in earlier times, as expressed in Jeronimo Lopez's statement in 1541: 'It is a most dangerous error to teach science to the Indians and still more to put the Bible and the holy scriptures in their hands . . . Many people in our Spain have been lost that way, and have invented a thousand heresies' (Johnson, 1976, p. 406). Today, a Latin American theologian can write, by contrast, 'It is no exaggeration to say that the poor and the oppressed have the most rightful "ownership" of the Bible and are in the most adequate context to re-read it' (Croatto, 1982, p. 59). The lively encounter of the poor with Scripture, arising out of a conviction that the Bible has meaning for today and provides the essential clues for right discerning of the signs of the times takes place not so much in lecture rooms as in slum congregations, small Bible study groups and what are known as 'base communities'. The poor and powerless, it is argued, have privileged access to the teaching of the Bible. It is easier for them to understand than for the rich and powerful.

The atmosphere of this encounter may be savoured in Ernesto Cardenal's remarkable books *The Gospel in Solentiname* (Cardenal, 1977–82). These volumes consist of Bible studies by a tiny congregation of fishermen and peasants in Nicaragua, tape-recorded by Cardenal, their parish priest. These were poor people, and they came to the Bible in the expectation that it contained Good News for them, and with the belief that it was written largely by people like them. They neither looked for nor appeared to experience the gigantic cultural gulf between the world of the Bible and the world of today which Dennis Nineham and others find so daunting. They come directly to the text, reading and discussing it in the light of their experience, always seeking the meaning for today, for themselves and for their society. The Bible studies are often marked not only by an extraordinary simplicity but also by a profundity and ability to penetrate into the meaning of a passage which is truly remarkable. The various participants bring their own slants, prejudices and ideological orientations to the studies, and are conscious of doing so, but within the group a great deal of mutual correction and balancing occurs as each listens and responds to what others have found in the passage. Cardenal, the parish priest, is the only participant who knows much of critical biblical scholarship. He does not speak often and he does not dominate the discussion. His contributions are models of how scholarship may serve the people's exploration of Scripture, rather than taking interpretation out of their hands. He enables and encourages them to probe, and gently dissuades them from entering dead-ends or pondering untenable interpretations. This is sound scholarship, contributed modestly and constructively. Cardenal appears to believe that a knowledge of biblical criticism on its own does not give one the ability to read the Bible aright; he will listen intently and often defer to the reading of those 'on the underside of history'.

What is happening in the course of these Bible studies in Solentiname is more than an attempt to interpret one's situation in the light of the Bible. Individually and as a community, the congregation is *possessing* the Bible, relating the biblical story to their contemporary story. They live *within* the story in a way which is hard for Westerners to appreciate, not so much, they would suggest, because Westerners are secularized as because they are so prosperous and powerful, whereas the Bible is largely a book written by and for the poor and the powerless. They will not allow the 'experts', the professionals, to claim a monopoly of the interpretation of Scripture, for this is a function and a responsibility of the whole people of God. But this way of reading Scripture is relevant to all:

> Reading the Bible with the eyes of the poor is a different thing from reading it with the eyes of a man with a full belly. If it is read in the light of the experience and hopes of the oppressed, the Bible's revolutionary themes – promise, exodus, ressurection and spirit – come alive. The way in which the history of Israel and the history of Christ blend with that of the hungry and oppressed

is quite different from the way in which they have often been linked with the history of the mighty and rich!

(Moltmann, 1978, p. 17)

There are, of course, dangers – of using the Bible simply to confirm one's ideological commitments, of disregarding the difficulties arising from the differences of historical context, of rejecting scholarly exegesis in favour of a purely subjective interpretation. But there are also exciting possibilities when people read the Bible convinced that it can give guidance for faithful praxis and is only really accessible to those who are committed to such Christian praxis. Carlos Mesters uses a telling analogy: 'We read the Bible something like the wealthy car owner who looks out over the top of his car and sees a nice chrome finish. The common people read the Bible something like the mechanic who looks up and sees a very different view of the same car' (in Torres and Eagleson, 1981, p. 207). Both views have their own validity, but are determined by the social position of the interpreter. The 'owner's' interest is aesthetic and utilitarian: he wants a vehicle that gets him there and serves his purposes, while looking good. The 'mechanic' is more involved with the inside, with the dynamics, of the vehicle; he does not *use* it but relates his praxis to its workings. Analogies should not be pressed too far, of course, but from this one there certainly arises the suggestion that the prosperous and the scholarly should pay attention to how the Bible appears to the poor and the weak and the uneducated, for the scholar's view and the scholar's reading is circumscribed by his social position.

Mesters, in his discussion of the use of the Bible in Basic Christian Communities in Brazil, speaks of the Bible as *history* for the people, and also as a mirror. It allows and encourages them to identify themselves with the Bible story, much as Jews through the ritual recital of the exodus story at Passover affirm their identity by taking possession of this story as *their* story, dovetailing together their personal histories and this primordial history, finding through *anamnesis* that the past lives powerfully in the present. Mesters describes how the Bible gives Brazilian peasants 'a new way of seeing':

They feel at home with the Bible and begin to link it with their lives. So we get something very interesting. They are mixing life in with the Bible, and the Bible in with life. One helps them to interpret the other. And often the Bible is what starts them developing a more critical awareness of reality. They say, for example, 'We are Abraham! *We* are in Egypt! *We* are in bondage! *We* are David!'

(in Torres and Eagleson, 1981, p. 206)

How closely parallel this is to the Passover *Haggada*: *We* were Pharaoh's slaves in Egypt, and the Lord our God brought us forth with a mighty hand and an outstretched arm. And if the Holy One, Blessed by He, had not brought our forefathers forth from Egypt, then we, our children, and our children's children would still be slaves in Egypt' (Glatzer, 1969, p. 23).

A similar attitude to the Bible lies at the root of the fascinating Minjung theology of Korea (Commission on Theological Concerns, 1983). The Minjung are the ordinary people of Korea, for long the victims of economic, cultural and political oppression, first by the Japanese and then by homegrown dictatorships. They tell the story of their sufferings and their hopes through poetry, myth, drama and dance. A century ago, missionaries translated the Bible into Hangul, the language of the Minjung, rather than Japanese or one of the other languages of the powerful. The Minjung almost immediately seized on the Bible story as their story; the exodus and the sufferings of Jesus became events in their history; the Bible gave them clues to discern the working of God in their times; they instinctively believed that the Gospel concerned both the religious and the political dimensions of life; and they refused to separate the destiny of the Christian community from that of the Korean people as a whole. The Minjung identify with the *ochlos*, the multitude, the people who were as sheep without a shepherd and who thronged around Jesus. For they were those on whom Jesus had compassion, the rejected ones who found acceptance with him. Thus, the Minjung discovered in Scripture a 'mirror' or system of symbols to interpret their historical experience, and motivation to seek the Kingdom of God and his justice above all else.

In Minjung theology, as in Latin American liberation

theology, there is not a rejection of biblical scholarship as such, but rather a suspicion of Western biblical scholarship, particularly when it is detached from the life and questions of the church of the poor. This is linked with a conviction that the purpose of scholarship is to enable, monitor and deepen the people's possession of Scripture and their faithful responsive praxis

THE LIMITS OF WESTERN BIBLICAL SCHOLARSHIP

The popular repossession of the Bible which underlies liberation theology, and the ways of reading the Bible which are characteristic of it, suggest that there are major limitations in Western biblical studies, some of which we will mention briefly.

First, liberation theology stresses the subtle and pervasive influence of the social context on the way in which the Bible is read, the social position of the interpreter deeply affecting how the text is handled and understood. Scholarship has been in recent years productive of rich insights into how the social context, and in particular the needs of the early Christian community, influenced the writing of the New Testament, but strangely blind to ways in which the social and economic context, the class position and the interests of the exegete affect the reading of Scripture – positively and negatively. As a form critic, Rudolph Bultmann had a peculiar sensitivity to the ways in which the social context shaped the composition of the New Testament. This makes all the more strange his failure to examine the possibility that the social context of the *reader* influences the way the text is read. There is a profound irony in the fact that Bultmann wrote his immensely influential essay on the New Testament and mythology in 1941 when the baneful influence of the mythology of Nazism was at its height, but does not allow this fact to cloud in any way his rather sunny view of the rationality of the modern world. It is as if he were attempting to detach himself from the dreadful realities of the day and relate his reading of the Bible to a different, gentler, but unreal, world inhabited by conscientious and slightly sceptical secular scholars. The essay reveals no clues to its true *sitz im Leben*. However, in reality, the social context and the social position of the interpreter affects the reading of Scripture both positively and negatively; they may illuminate some things and obscure others.

Secondly, liberation theology stresses that there is no such thing as an objective, final and complete reading of Scripture, although this does not mean that a text is capable of bearing any meaning we care to put upon it. Liberation theology uses the tools of modern biblical scholarship to question the claim of some academic biblical studies to objectivity and impartiality in interpretation. An impressive and easily accessible example of this is José P. Miranda's early book, very misleadingly entitled *Marx and the Bible* (Miranda, 1977). Miranda has an elaborate exegetical armoury and, although many of his arguments and conclusions are suspect, he has demonstrated pretty convincingly that at several key points distinguished academic commentators have been blind to certain emphases in the text. It is necessary to keep this in mind when considering the charge so often preferred against the liberation theologians of being selective, precritical and simplistic in their use of Scripture – a charge which seems increasingly threadbare as they produce more substantial biblical works, find allies in the Western academic establishment of the standing of Norman Gottwald, Gerd Theissen and Robin Scroggs, and are beginning to be regarded as pioneers of the sociological and materialist styles of exegesis (Gottwald, 1983). 'Objective neutrality', argues Walter Wink, 'requires a sacrifice of the very questions the Bible seeks to answer . . . Objectivism is not simply in error, however. It is a false consciousness' (Wink, 1975, pp. 3, 6). He presses his charge thus:

It pretends to be unbiased when in fact the methodology carries with it a heavy rationalistic weight which by inner necessity tends towards the reduction of irrational, subjective or emotional data to insignificance or invisibility. It pretends to a search for 'assured results', 'objective knowledge', when in fact the method presumes radical epistemological doubt which by definition devours each new spawn of 'assured results' as a guppy swallows her children, It pretends to suspend evaluations, which is simply impossible, since research proceeds on the basis of questions asked and a ranked priority in their asking. But such judgements presuppose a system of values and an ontology of meanings which not only give weight to the questions but make it possible to ask them at all.

(Wink, 1975, p. 6f)

We must therefore ask of every exegesis in whose interests, for whom and by whom is it being done.

Liberation theology reminds us that the Bible is constantly used or abused as a weapon for the defence of group or individual interests. This is a religious process well known to anthropologists, which can work in both directions. In India, for instance, untouchable castes often have myths characteristically describing how in the distant past they had had a higher status than today, and had been free from oppression, how by trickery they had been reduced to their present degradation and how a restoration of their dignity and liberty was sure to come shortly. In some cases, when untouchable castes have been converted to Christianity, they have drawn close parallels between their myths of this kind and the Bible story, as the Minjung did in Korea (Forrester, 1980). Other processes are used to protect interests against challenge from the Bible, and here sometimes scholarship is called in to assist, as Kierkegaard suggests in a naughty but perceptive passage:

> Suppose that in the New Testament it were written, for example (a thing we can at least suppose), that every man should have $100,000 ... Do you believe that then there would be any question of a commentary? – or not rather that everyone would say: That is easy enough to understand, there is absolutely no need of a commentary, for God's sake, let us be delivered from any commentary ...
>
> But what actually is written in the New Testament (about the narrow way, about dying to the world) is not a bit more difficult to understand than that about the $100,000. The difficulty lies elsewhere, in the fact that it is not to our liking – and therefore, we must have commentaries and professors and commentaries.
>
> It is to get rid of doing God's will that we have invented learning ... we shield ourselves by hiding behind tomes.

(Lowrie, 1962, p. 539)

There is a proper use, as well as an abuse, of the Bible as a weapon. Once again, an important step towards a responsible handling of Scripture is to be conscious of the processes, and the opportunities and dangers they present.

POLITICAL HERMENEUTICS

Political theology challenges the common assumption that the Bible, despite its concern with history and its concentration on a particular people and specific events, is chiefly important because it generates truths of universal validity and timeless doctrines. The Bible, in other words, has the primary function of illuminating the understanding and challenging the intellect. And in as far as the Bible is seen as a book of history at all, it is largely the history of ideas, or the development of doctrines that are to be found within its pages. It is this idealist reading of the Bible – which was the reason why Nietzsche denounced Christianity as 'Platonism for the people' – that is contested by recent materialistist and political readings of the Bible. Such approaches stress that the interpretation of the Bible must be closely related to praxis. We cannot read the Bible aright without some understanding of the demands and problems of the praxis of the community out of which the Biblical documents emerged. And the Bible can only be read aright in a church community which is in fact engaged in true Christian praxis. Neither God nor the Bible can be properly understood in a society which turns a blind eye to injustice (Miranda, 1977, pp. 44–5).

But that does not mean that it is impossible to read the Bible except in a perfectly just society, but that only those whose praxis centres on the doing of justice may read the Bible aright. When the Bible is used 'as if it were a special constable's handbook – an opium dose for keeping beasts of burden patient while they were being overloaded – a mere book to keep the poor in order' (Charles Kingsley), it is radically distorted. The Bible is not primarily a 'religious' book: it is about justice, and therefore it requires political hermeneutic (Miranda, 1977, p. 93). In order to understand the Bible aright we need to allow it to challenge and illuminate our praxis. No wholly non-political reading is possible, as Severino Croatto argues:

> When people criticise the political reading of the Bible done by liberation theology, they are taking a political option from a concrete praxis with its own political overtones, and a hermeneutical option. They 'close' or exclude a political reading because they have opted for another reading, which in fact is equally political though with a different content. Their criticism, moreover, forgets that the Bible is a text 'produced' in hermeneutical correlation with the socio-historical praxis of a whole nation and that is, therefore, pregnant with politics. The Bible is the Word of God for a people seeking to fulfil its *historical* project of peace, justice, faithfulness, love, welfare and freedom.
> (Croatto, 1982, pp. 60–1)

Liberation theology's skirmish with academic biblical scholarship has meanwhile contributed to the development of a good deal of significant writing on a new political, or materialist, or sociological hermeneutic, characteristically assuming that the exegete should be politically committed and making much use of the social sciences, particularly in their Marxist versions. In France, for example, Fernando Belo published *A Materialist Reading of the Gospel of Mark* (Belo, 1974; English trans. 1981). Belo is a Portuguese laicized priest of immense learning, who is deeply involved in the class struggle. His book is a vast, complex and magisterial production. His thought, and the materialist reading of Scripture which he inaugurated, has been made more easily accessible by one of his collaborators, Michel Clévenot, in *Materialist Approaches to the Bible* (1976; English trans. 1985). In Germany, meanwhile, Gerd Theissen's studies of the early church and the work of the contributors to *God of the Lowly: Socio-historical Interpretations of the Bible* (Schotroff and Stegemann, 1979; English trans. 1984) took a similar line; and in the United States, Norman Gottwald's vast *The Tribes of Jahweh: A Sociology of the Religion of Liberated Israel, 1250–1050 BCE* (1979) was a major landmark, presenting a Marxist reading of Old Testament history. Gottwald has now edited an important reader, *The Bible and Liberation: Political and Social Hermeneutics* (1983) which examines ways of reading the Bible which 'bring to light the actual social struggles of our biblical ancestors and . . . locate the human and religious resources they drew upon in the midst of these struggles' in the hope that this will enable us 'to tap the biblical social struggles and religious understandings as important resources for directing us in the social struggles we are at presently engaged in' (Gottwald, 1983, p. 2).

Belo's reading of Mark is not materialist in the ethical sense, but materialist in as far as he starts from concrete realities rather than from ideas, taking both the economic context in which the Gospel was written and the materiality of the text with profound seriousness. By this last he means the fact that the Gospel was the product of people in a particular social and economic situation. Because he believes that Marxism provides the most illuminating analysis of social formations and social conflicts, he sets out to read Mark in the light of Marx. The point of departure, as Clévenot says, is 'the present struggles in which we are involved, so that we can re-read the texts that have woven our history and free them from those who have used them to legitimize their own power' (Clévenot, 1985, p. xi). The Gospel is to be studied as a whole; there is an implicit suggestion that some biblical scholarship, by chopping the text up into 'periscopes' for study, not only misses the coherent message but is following the adage 'divide and conquer' in order to control the text.

We are not surprised to discover that Belo finds Mark to be a subversive book, or rather that the praxis of Jesus and his disciples, as described there, is deeply subversive of the established ordering of things. The praxis of Jesus questions fundamental ideas on purity and pollution. Jesus reaches out to the impure and the excluded to draw them into a fellowship, which is itself a protest against the hierarchical ordering of society. He subverts the symbolic order of contemporary Judaism, and the economic, political and religious dominance which has its seat in the temple. Jesus is more radical than the Zealots in as far as he does not seek a restoration of a purified Jewish state and temple, and rejects their strategy of armed revolt against Rome. Jesus is executed for wishing to tear down the temple and build a new and quite different one; the Zealots are willing to die for the temple. Thus we have in the Gospel of Mark an account of the radical, subversive praxis of Jesus. But already in the Gospel and the New Testament begins the attempt to tone down and blunt the challenge of this radical praxis, so that following Jesus gradually becomes regarded as an individual, a religious and a conformist matter.

George V. Pixley, a Mexican Baptist Old Testament scholar, has produced a remarkable book, *God's Kingdom* (1981), which has affinities both with Gottwald's work on ancient Israel and Belo's study of Mark. Pixley finds 'a significant liberating tradition within sacred texts' (Pixley, 1981, p. 104). This is by no means the *only* thing that is to be found in Scripture; he would agree with Belo that there is much in the Bible which tones down or obscures the strain of liberation. But it must be to this element in Scripture that we turn if we start, as Pixley does, with the question whether the Kingdom of God is good news for the poor. The Kingdom, Pixley argues, is a key concept in the Old Testament which provides the necessary background for understanding why Jesus uses the coming of the Kingdom as the heart of his message. In abstract and general terms, the Kingdom means a society of justice, equality and abundance. But in the Bible it is always presented in terms of some specific 'historical project' or embodiment. Some of these projects Pixley sees as oppressive – for instance, the attempt to embody the Kingdom in the Old Testament monarchy, or in priestly society and the centralized worship of the temple. But others, most notably the project of tribal Israel, the pilgrim people of God and the strategy of Jesus and his group of disciples, were highly liberative. Jesus travelled around Galilee gathering a band of disciples around him who expressed in their life together the egalitarian principles of God's Kingdom. The multitude was seen as the beneficiary of the coming Kingdom, and they were the special care of Jesus and the disciples, who fed, taught and healed them. Moving from place to place, the Jesus movement repeatedly encountered opposition, particularly from the religious and social establishment, the 'scribes and Pharisees' of the gospels. The strategy of Jesus then involves his 'setting his face steadfastly towards Jerusalem', there to confront the system of oppression at its most powerful point, the temple:

By attacking the banking and commercial aspects of the temple they were not attacking a minor sideshow. This was fundamental to the class system. It was by means of the trade and the taxes collected in the temple that the priests extracted the surplus labour of the peasants. Several of the teaching incidents put by the gospel writers in the context of the temple in that week have to do with money (Caesar's coin, the widow's mite, Judas Iscariot's bargain with the priests). The economic base of the temple's domination was challenged by Jesus and his movement.

(Pixley, 1981, p. 75)

The temple, rather than Rome, was the primary antagonist for the Jesus movement.

With the death of Jesus came the internationalization of God's Kingdom, a new project, or rather a series of projects, some of which were liberative and others oppressive:

In the first century of the Christian era, under the impact of Roman oppression, God's kingdom again became the inspiration for rebellion and the promise of liberation. Still, none of the strategies to make the kingdom a reality was successful. Jesus and his movement did not achieve the mass support needed to set in motion their historical project before it was cut off by Jesus' crucifixion. The Zealots had their moment of glory when they consolidated the rebel forces in an armed struggle, but they were defeated by the superior military power of Rome. And the Pharisees and their rabbinical successors have continued to wait for the Kingdom for centuries. From the messianic Jesus movement there arose a universal, spiritual, and individualistic religion that offers inner salvation to oppressed men and women within various class systems.

(Pixley, 1981, p. 102)

All this demonstrates that there is indeed 'a significant liberating tradition' within the Bible, alongside much else that is oppressive. This is, or may be, a significant resource for the poor and the oppressed in their struggle for liberation today. But 'only experience will tell if the biblical kingdom of God can be truly good news for the poor, the exploited workers of Latin America' (Pixley, 1981, p. 104). Thus Pixley challenges Christians, and particularly exegetes, to turn back to the Bible as a resource for liberation. But he makes no claim that his reading is final, authoritative or comprehensive. It is offered in order that it might be tested – against the text, and as a resource for liberating praxis.

Liberation theology thus addresses rather different questions to the Bible from those of academic biblical scholarship. It asks what there is in the Bible story to which we may relate; how we may dovetail our story and the story of our people with the Bible story of the People of God; what there is in Scripture that we may appropriate and use in today's struggles. It emphasizes the similarities rather than the differences between modern situations and the situations out of which biblical narratives emerge, so that it is not at all surprised when the ordinary people of Korea identify so easily with the multitude that thronged around Jesus. It uses the techniques of biblical scholarship in an increasingly responsible and scholarly manner, but calls for a new sensitivity to ways in which the social context, interests and commitments of the exegete affect the reading of Scripture, for good or ill. It suggests a servant role for academic scholarship: its task is to encourage and guide rather than dominate the people's reading of the Bible; above all, the experts are not to take away from the people the right and the responsibility of interpreting Scripture for themselves. A wise scholar will listen attentively to the people's reading in the expectation that they may have insights into the meaning of the text that are hidden from him. Liberation theology is not profoundly concerned that it has been accused of selectivity in its use of Scripture because, it responds, all interpretations are selective; and it is proper for a plurality of interpretations to be debated and tested within both the household of faith and the academy.

Liberation theology has reaffirmed the bearing of commitment to praxis on biblical interpretation. The hermeneutic circle, as developed by Juan Luis Segundo and others, starts from a suspicion of received ideologies and interpretations and a commitment to praxis, understood in both religious and political terms. Out of experience of committed engagement, questions arise which are addressed to received understandings of life, of theology and of the Bible. This critical questioning leads to new interpretations, new ways of understanding the Bible, which in turn reshape and deepen praxis and commitment.

This linking of praxis and interpretation is a salutary challenge to those who treat the Bible simply as a classic of literature, to be studied much as we would study Homer. Moreover, it is hermeneutically more plausible than the approach which attempts *first* to get the exegesis right, in a more or less timeless way, detached from the situation, and *then* to apply the exegesis to life.

We have traced in broad outline what cannot be seen as other than a major retreat in Western theology from the use of the Bible in social and political matters. We then saw, with liberation theology, an unexpected and thoroughgoing reversal of this process. This reversal should encourage Western theologians to look again at the bearing of the Bible on the issues of the day. But two problems need to be mentioned in conclusion. First, the repossession of Scripture by the people in lands where the vast majority are poor and relatively uneducated is surely less problematic than a similar project in wealthy, radically secularized post-Protestant industrial societies. And, secondly, the guidance which the liberation theologians find in the Bible relates mainly to the goals and hopes of the poor and the powerless. This is, of course, of the greatest importance. But other, and awkward, problems arise in considering the kind of help that might be derived from the Bible for decision-makers facing the dilemmas and the ambiguities involved in the responsible use of power. Here the liberation theologians have little help to offer, except to introduce suspicion of concentrations of irresponsible power. And that, as we shall see later, ia a vitally important contribution and challenge.

CHAPTER 5

A Political Christ?

FASCINATION AND PERPLEXITY

For twenty centuries each successive generation has been fascinated and perplexed by the figure of Jesus of Nazareth. This has been as true in politics as in art, in personal piety as in popular culture. Outside the Church as well as within, there have been countless endeavours to interpret and relate to this figure who walked the streets of Galilee and Judaea in the early years of the Christian era and has been understood in countless ways ever since those times. Already in the New Testament there are to be found a number of different and more or less coherent christologies, or attempts to make theological sense of Jesus. And many others were developed later: some labelled orthodox and others dismissed as heresies; some, like that to be found in the Qu'rān or Mahatma Gandhi's teaching on Jesus, interpretations through the prism of another faith; some, like the rock operas *Godspell* and *Jesus Christ Superstar*, presenting Jesus in the music and idiom of modern pop culture. It would seem that even in a sceptical and secular age, it is not possible to forget Jesus of Nazareth or escape from his spell. This figure continues to fascinate and perplex, and the rich and confusing profusion of interpetations goes on increasing at an amazing rate.

From the beginning, there has been a political dimension in the interpretation of Jesus which has sometimes been so heavily overlaid that it is almost invisible and at other times appears boldly. In affirming that Jesus is Lord, believers were appropriating the Old Testament belief in the Kingship of Yahweh and ascribing precisely that authority and status to Jesus. Simultaneously, of course, the confession of Jesus as Lord was a challenge to secular kingship and political authority: in Jesus, they affirmed, we see the true pattern of lordship, the standard against which all earthly authority is to be measured. Jesus cuts the powers down to size, he renders their pretensions relative. Their claims to divine status, to some kind of ultimacy, dissolve before him. The confession was proclaiming that Jesus *is* a king, but in a far broader and more ultimate sense than that suggested by the superscription that Pilate attached to the Cross to indicate the charge for which Jesus was being executed: 'The King of the Jews' (Matt. 27: 37; Mark 15: 26; Luke 23: 38; John 19: 19).

And that label on the Cross of Jesus also points directly to one of the fundamental perplexities: how is it possible to confess that the crucified One is the King? The tension here is an intolerable one which cannot be sustained by a simple, traditionalist political theology, seeking an easy accommodation between divine and earthly authority. The question remains open whether it makes sense, and if so what sense, to affirm that Jesus reigns from the Cross. The attempts of iconography to ease the tension by depicting a serene, untroubled Jesus in kingly robes ruling from the Cross have not helped, precisely because they obscure the pain, degradation and shame of the execution of Jesus, and erase the irony of the superscription. The Crucified One belongs in the realm of politics as a sign of contradiction.

If we are to have an image of Jesus which is not simply a projection from a particular social context, it would seem wise to check against the Bible, to seek 'the historical Jesus', stripped from all theological adornment or time-limited interpretation. This was the endeavour of the century of German theology which Albert Schweitzer examined in his classic *The Quest of the Historical Jesus* (English trans. 1910). His depressing conclusion was that this vast expenditure of intellectual energy had produced portraits of Jesus which were largely self-portraits of their authors: liberal theologians produced a liberal Jesus, rationalist theologians produced a rationalist Jesus. It was, as Tyrell has suggested, like a man looking down a deep well very intently and then seeing far below in the dark waters his own face dimly reflected back to him. Those who claimed to have discovered 'the Jesus of history' presented a Jesus who never existed, 'a figure designed by rationalism, endowed with life by liberalism, and clothed by modern theology in an historical garb' (Schweitzer, 1910, p. 396). The central problem, Schweitzer taught, is that Jesus is forever rooted in a world radically alien from ours, a world full of expectations of an imminent end, the battleground of cosmic forces, with a worldview that modern people regard as primitive. He cannot be plucked from his context and transplanted to ours (remember that Schweitzer was writing before the nineteenth-century liberal optimism had been shattered by the First World War). Jesus is, and must remain, 'a stranger to our time'.

Schweitzer did not believe that the end was at hand; he held Jesus and his contemporaries to be mistaken in their expectation. But he understood Jesus as an ever-present Lord who calls for our allegiance. In his well-known conclusion to his book, Schweitzer says that the Jesus who is 'One unknown' still comes to us as 'an imperious ruler':

> He comes to us as One unknown, without a name, as of old, by the lakeside He came to those men who knew Him not. He speaks to us the same word: 'Follow thou me!' and sets us to the tasks which He has to fulfil for our time. He commands. And to those who obey him, whether they be wise or simple, He will reveal Himself in the toils, the conflicts, the sufferings which they shall pass through in His fellowship, and, as an ineffable mystery, they shall learn in their own experience Who He is.
>
> (Schweitzer, 1910, p. 401)

This much can be known of Jesus: he is a ruler whose call and whose command still come to us. In practical response rather than in detached speculation, we come to know him as he is today. For Schweitzer this meant the call to serve in the mission hospital in Lambarene in West Africa. Schweitzer's Jesus is a ruler who makes radical demands, and who (as Schweitzer's own praxis testifies) has a special care for the weak, the poor and the sick; this is a challenging, disturbing Jesus. One might contrast this with Jack T Sanders' conclusion that the call of Jesus also is imprisoned in the first century, and no longer relevant in the modern world, so that we are set free to work out our own style of life, without reference to Jesus or to the roots of the Christian tradition. For Sanders, the imperious ruler is not accessible in the modern world. His command can no longer be heard. (Sanders, 1975, p. 130).

No sooner had Schweitzer's argument that Jesus was embedded in an alien eschatological world so that he could be no more than a stranger in our day been assimilated than the Western world was engulfed in a period of turmoil which made the eschatological Jesus Schweitzer had discovered intelligible and relevant for many. For Barth and his school, the redis-covered eschatological Jesus was of immense political rele-vance; they sought to hear and respond to his command, as the ruler of the whole of life, as one political crisis succeeded another. Bultmann and his followers proclaimed that the true Jesus is not the shadowy historical figure but the preached Christ, whose challenge and command comes to each individual anew in the crisis of eschatological decision. This Jesus had little apparent bearing on the political world; his realm was the heart. Bultmann, the existentialist theologian, produced a Jesus who was both unpolitical and unhistorical; but Bultmann, the form critic, through his painstaking efforts to interpret the details of the Gospel narratives in the light of the needs and interests of the earliest Christian community opened possi-bilities, which others are exploring, for the development of a political theology and a picture of Jesus which takes full account of the modern social context as well (Sölle, 1974).

More recent academic research has suggested possibilities of a new quest for the historical Jesus of a rather different sort. And people concerned to translate for our day the early Church's message about Jesus, especially those who are con-vinced that this message is addressed particularly to the poor, the weak, the hungry and those who seek first the Kingdom of

God and his righteousness, are turning with a new expectation to the biblical scholars for assistance.

THE MARXISTS' JESUS

Although he believed that in principle the question of religion had already been explained, or rather explained away, Marx still gave considerable attention to the discussion of religion in general and Christianity in particular. Religion for him involved a distorted worldview which needed to be removed before people could see reality and see it whole. But for Marxists it is not enough to adopt the old rationalist view that religion is false and therefore must be disposed of. Religion requires to be explained; we need to know what functions religion serves and account for its continuing influence and hold on the minds and hearts of many. In well-known words, Marx declared:

> Religious suffering is at the same time an expression of real suffering and a protest against real suffering. Religion is the sigh of the oppressed creature, the feeling of a heartless world, and the soul of soulless circumstances. It is the opium of the people.
>
> The abolition of religion as the illusory happiness of the people is the demand for their real happiness. The demand to give up the illusions about their condition is a demand to give up a condition that demands illusion. The criticism of religion is therefore the germ of the criticism of the valley of tears whose halo is religion.
>
> Criticism has plucked the imaginary flowers from the chains not so that man may bear chains without any imagination or comfort, but so that he may throw away the chains and pluck living flowers. The criticism of religion disillusions man so that he may think, act, and fashion his own reality as a disillusioned man come to his senses; so that he may revolve around himself as his real sun. Religion is only the illusory sun which revolves around man as long as he does not revolve around himself.
>
> (quoted in McLellan, 1977, p. 63)

Only when religion has been disposed of can the real roots of human distress be tackled. And the harmful effects of a religious attitude penetrate very deeply.

In *Capital* Marx argues that a fundamental defect of the capitalist system is that it encourages a kind of idolatry, a religious
attitude of reverence towards *things*, the phenomenon he calls
'fetishism of commodities'. Capitalism indeed depends on this
religious attitude, and Christianity, which, following Hegel, he
sees as the epitome of religion as such, has allowed itself to be
taken over and transformed into the religion of capital. It no
longer has the prophetic resources to confront this idolatry, and
prophecy must now become a purely secular critique.

Marx and Engels were interested in religion, but significantly
silent about Jesus. Marx, at least from the writing of his
doctoral dissertation in 1841 on *The Natural Philosophy of
Democritus and the Natural Philosohpy of Epicurus*, took the
figure of Prometheus from Greek mythology as a prominent
symbol for his own self-understanding. 'Prometheus,' he wrote,
'is the noblest of saints and martyrs in the calendar of philosophy' (Marx and Engels, 1957 edn, p. 15). It was Prometheus,
the rebel who stole the fire of the gods, who stood for human
dignity and freedom against divine oppression, rather than
Jesus, even the Jesus who 'came to cast fire upon the earth'
(Luke 12: 49), and was regarded by some of the early Fathers as
the true Prometheus, whom Marx adopted as a kind of model
(Bentley, 1982, p. 102).

The first serious Marxist account of Jesus only came in 1908,
when Karl Kautsky published *The Foundations of Christianity*,
in which he attempted to explain the rise of Christianity and the
figure of Jesus. He was not convinced that Jesus had ever
existed, but tried to take account of this possibly entirely
mythological figure in terms of the social forces of the first century, and the religion which looks to Jesus as its founder. A later
Marxist whose own work we shall be discussing shortly commends Kautsky's book as trail-blazing:

Kautsky's work is particularly valuable . . . in that it was the
first book in the field of the study of Jesus to be based on the
spirit of strict determinism: Christianity is seen here not as the
work of a God who steps down from heaven, or as the result of
sheer human design, the intentions of the apostles or the visions
of fanatical women, but as a real answer of millions of men to the
crisis of their time. The origin of Christianity, therefore, does not

lie in any kind of miraculous revelation, or even in a moral
miracle; on the contrary, in the given social situation it would
rather have been a miracle if Christianity had *not* come into
being.

(Machovec, 1976, pp. 216–17)

Kautsky depicts the intellectual decay of the ancient world and
the economic problems which appeared incapable of an economic solution, and therefore encouraged the masses to turn in
hope to religion and pin their faith on the death and resurrection
of Jesus. On this basis, Kautsky gives detailed attention to
many of the Gospel stories, sometimes treating them in an
almost literalist way. Kautsky agrees with Engels that a religion which had 'dominated by far the greater part of civilised
humanity for 1800 years' must have more to it than 'nonsense
gleaned together by frauds'; at the least, it is necessary to
explain why this particular piece of nonsense was preferred by
such vast masses of people to all the other nonsensical interpretations which were on offer. Engels and Kautsky agree in
seeing early Christianity as essentially a working-class movement, and both quote with evident approval Renan's famous
statement that 'If I wanted to give you an idea of the early
Christian communities I would tell you to look at a local section
of the International Working Men's Association' (Marx and
Engels, 1957 edn, pp. 194, 315). Jesus emerges as a shadowy
prophetic figure who inspired a community which experimented
with forms of primitive communism and preached a socially
revolutionary Gospel until it was sucked into 'the system'
under Constantine.

In more recent times, there has been a significant revival of
interest in Jesus among Marxists, not on the part of official
ideologues, but by rather independent-minded thinkers who
have often been dismissed as heretics by the more orthodox. In
a class of his own stands the towering and independent figure of
Ernst Bloch (1885–1977). Bloch played a leading role in the
reconsideration of historical materialism among German
Marxists in the 1920s and early 1930s. Hitler's coming to power
forced him to emigrate, and he spent the war years in the United
States, where he wrote his monumental *The Principle of Hope*
(1959; English trans. 1986). After the war, Bloch returned to

teach philosophy in Leipzig, but his unremitting challenge to the rigid Marxist orthodoxy of the time made him unacceptable in East Germany and in 1961 he moved to Tübingen in West Germany. From his first book, *The Spirit of Utopia* (1918) onwards, and especially in *Atheism in Christianity* (1968; English trans. 1972), Bloch showed himself as centrally concerned with the biblical roots of expectations of a better future. It was for him precisely the eschatological emphasis in Scripture, which Schweitzer and the liberals found so inaccessible, that was the great contribution of the Judaeo-Christian tradition to the world, to which even atheists and Marxists required to turn if they were to understand the roots and the implications of their own fundamental commitments.

German theologians, particularly Jürgen Moltmann and Wolfhart Pannenberg, found Bloch an indispensable dialogue partner in the 1960s; Moltmann's *The Theology of Hope* (1967) shows how profound was the influence of this atheist upon the development of Christian theology. Theologians, of course, required to contest Bloch's assertion that a hope which claimed to be a biblical hope was separable from God, that hope could thus be secularized without the loss of that which sustains it. Those who are 'without God in the world', Ephesians suggests, have 'no hope' (Eph. 2:12). But Christians welcomed more emphatically the fact that Bloch gave a central place in his analysis of hope to the figure of Jesus, arguing that both the historicity of Jesus and his eschatological expectation are of the greatest continuing importance. 'The stable, the carpenter's son, the visionary among simple people, the gallows at the end', he wrote, 'this is taken from historical stuff, not the golden stuff beloved of legend' (Bloch, 1986 edn, p. 1256). This historical figure (around whom much myth and legend has admittedly gathered) can only be understood in 'the framework of expectations' of the time, hopes which were quite specific to that period and that culture, yet of perennial significance. The actual life and Gospel of Jesus contrasted strongly with the expectations of the age. They resisted restriction to a spiritual and religious realm, or reduction to an ethnic hope. 'His *last, fearful supper, his despair in Gethsemane, his abandonment on the cross and his exclamations*: they do not accord with any legend of the Messiah-king, not even with that of the suffering Messiah' (Bloch, 1986 edn, p. 1259). Christianity therefore is 'essentially the imitation of a life on earth, not of a cult-image and its gnosis'.

This historical figure was notable for his special openness to the poor and despised, and for his rebellion against the powerful. There is a Promethean strain in Bloch's interpretation of Jesus, which does not sit altogether easily with the sources; for him Jesus and Job are both alike figures in rebellion against an authoritarian deity. For Bloch, Jesus on the Cross supplants God, henceforward God is Jesus – or, for an atheist, the figure of the historical Jesus fills the role that once was God's:

> A new god comes into being, one hitherto unheard of, who gives his blood for his children, who, as word become flesh, is capable of suffering the fate of death in a completely earthly way . . . Here a man, through the hubris of complete devotion, overhauled every idea of God to date; Jesus becomes a love of God such as has never been conceived in any god.
>
> (Bloch, 1986 edn, p. 1266)

This Jesus is the abiding ground for a rebellious hope which is this-worldly and transcendent as well, and provides vital clues to the nature and possibilities of human flourishing. Without dreams, hopes, promises, a truly human existence is impossible and we are trapped in the present. The story of Jesus and reflection upon that story provides one of the most potent and creatively disturbing longings that the world has known.

Two further Marxist interpretations of Jesus emerged from Czech scholars as the result of prolonged and constructive discussions between theologians and communist thinkers, particularly between 1956 and 1968 when the brief experiment in 'socialism with a human face', itself somewhat influenced by the Marxist–Christian dialogue, was brought to an abrupt end by Soviet intervention.

Milan Machovec, who was Professor of Philosophy at the Charles University in Prague, remarked in 1968: 'I would not be sorry at the demise of religion as such, but if I should live in a world which could forget totally the 'Jesus event' I would not

want to live at all' (Mojzes, 1978, p. 90). Machovec turns to the
figure of Jesus of Nazareth with openness and sympathy: his
'quest of the historical Jesus' is predicated upon a profound suspicion of the 'Christ of faith' and an endeavour to penetrate
behind what he regards as dogmatic and mythological distortion to discover the authentic historical figure. As a materialist, he finds form criticism, and the work of Rudolph Bultmann
in particular, an indispensable tool for investigating the
evidence. His whole approach is scholarly, honest and careful,
and it is a fascinating and impressive study, for the recovery of
an authentic understanding of Jesus is clearly of great importance to him. As he says himself, 'I write about Jesus with
enthusiasm and passion' (Machovec, 1976, p. 18).

Jesus, for Machovec, was not a Zealot nor a political liberator;
'his ambitions were vaster and more profound' (Machovec,
1976, p. 132), and the Kingdom that he proclaimed was more
than and other than even his disciples understood, Jesus opened
up a truly human future, and 'he embodied this lived future with
his own being' (Machovec, 1976, pp. 89–90): They saw in him a
man who already belonged to this coming Kingdom of God; they
saw what it meant to be 'full of grace', what it meant to be not
only a preacher but himself the product of his preaching, a child
of the future age to the marrow of his bones, (Machovec, 1976,
p. 90). The crucifixion was, in fact, the victory of Jesus, though
it was hard for the disciple to assimilate that a Calvary without
a parousia was other than a tragedy and an absurdity
(Machovec, 1976, p. 163). Machovec has more problems with the
resurrection. It is, he argues, strange and requiring explanation
that the Jesus movement did not come to an end with his death,
his disciples scattering and disappearing like the followers of
other executed prophets and holy men. How was this massive
disappointment overcome, how was the Cross turned into a
triumph, which was the birth of one of the world's great religions? How did a prophet whose predictions had failed come to
be worshipped and followed as a living Lord? Conscious decep-
tion, confusion or fraud cannot provide convincing explanations
for the genesis of the Easter faith: 'It needed true faith and profound conviction to preach Jesus as victorious in spite of the
scandal of his death on Calvary. Only genuine faith could be the

starting-point for the Christian mission' (Machovec, 1976, p. 165). None of the traditional materialist explanations for the Easter faith seems convincing to Machovec; he leaves the matter open, a tantalizing question which stands as an invitation to further dialogue: how do we understand this ultimate boundary event? And this dialogue, Machovec is clear, is a family discussion among Christians and Marxists who share a common history and heritage.

Another Czech philosopher, Vitezslav Gardavsky, published in 1966 and 1967 a series of articles defending an atheist position but suggesting that some useful lessons were to be learned from the Christian tradition and from the figure of Jesus. These articles were translated into English and published under the apt title *God Is Not Yet Dead* in 1973. Gardavsky turns to Jesus in order to nourish and enrich the modern atheistic communist position from what he sees as its historical roots, and also to challenge his Christian dialogue partners to be more faithful to the things that Jesus stands for. It is possible to understand Jesus without being religious, for he is:

> one of the models for human life, which during the course of history emerged as a new answer to the basic questions, as an alternative to the old and obsolete answers; the answer he put forward was so profound that it still has something to say to us today and to teach us – in spite of the number of times it has been distorted over the two thousand years since it first appeared, and in spite of all those occasions when it has been 'definitively' refuted.
>
> (Gardavsky, 1973, p. 36)

Gardavsky's approach is far more reductionist than is Machovec's, but he sees the figure of Jesus as an important symbol in two particular ways. First, he shows us what is possible for human beings. 'His own actions show us that it is really possible: man is capable of performing miracles. Miracles are performed. They are the nodal points in the web of history, the junctures where something unique takes place, an incident which can never be repeated' (Gardavsky, 1973, p. 49). Secondly, the figure of Jesus is a constant reminder of the centrality of love. And this is of particular importance when we remember that Gardavsky is not simply defending atheism, but reassessing it in the light of the kind of oppression, rigidity and despotism which atheistic communism had generated under Stalin. The 'socialism with a human face' which was sought in the brief Czech Spring was clearly influenced by the figure of Jesus.

Roger Garaudy, a leading ideologue of the French Communist Party, was also deeply involved in Christian–Marxist dialogue. Concerned that he was moving away from communist orthodoxy, the French Communist Party expelled him in 1970. In 1975 he proclaimed himself a Christian. His conversion meant renouncing atheism, but not communism for he now believed that communism needed to be sustained and renewed through Christian faith. Faith is the source of hope and of revolutionary activity: 'Faith engenders not resignation but impatience and conflict with the world. It wrenches one way from what is given' (Garaudy, 1976, p. 96). Religion is now not so much the opium of the people as 'the expression of real distress and the protest against real distress' (Marx and Engels, 1957, edn p. 42). And Jesus? 'He is the fully human man whose every action teaches us to look to ultimate objectives. One can know nothing of God except through this man who intercedes and calls' (Garaudy, 1976, p. 96). 'In him the God of distant transcendence entered into the daily history of men. He made him a breaker of idols and chains, a bypasser of boundaries, one who destroyed taboos and placed himself beyond justice, good and evil in the name of a love that transcended all historical limits' (Garaudy, 1976, p. 91). Marxism, he concludes, can only be an authentic liberating force if it incorporates this insight into the meaning of true humanity.

THE JESUS OF POPULAR PIETY

There is often a sharp distinction between what theologians are teaching about Jesus and what people actually believe, between the formally articulated theology which is studied in the university and the seminary, and the implicit theology which is expressed in the piety of the people. Protestants have a traditional suspicion of popular religion as having an almost inbuilt tendency towards superstition, and see it as something which should be controlled and purified from above by those qualified to do so. Catholics have been perhaps a trifle more tolerant. Occasionally, Catholic theologians have seen popular religion as a subject for theological reflection, but more commonly they have simply accepted even its more bizarre expressions as some kind of necessary concession to the inherent dottiness of human nature. And whereas Protestants have inclined to supress or exclude many manifestations of popular religion as superstitious, Catholics have been more accommodating, allowing popular religion a place, if not a powerful and influential one, within the accepted forms of expression of the Christian faith.

It is therefore not surprising that Latin American Roman Catholic and Protestant theologians should view popular images of Jesus *sympathetically*, but not *uncritically*. And since liberation theologians see a central part of their vocation as providing a voice for the voiceless masses of the people, it is only natural that they sometimes regard popular images of Jesus as resources for theology and devote attention to examining closely popular and largely inarticulate christologies (Comblin, 1985). On the other hand, there are liberation theologians, both Roman Catholics and Protestant, who have a fundamental suspicion of 'religion' in general, and forms of popular piety and cultic activity in particular, which is very reminiscent of the strain in Protestant theology whose greatest twentieth-century exponents were Karl Barth and Dietrich Bonhoeffer. For them, the perennial temptation is for Christianity to be sucked into being a 'religion' like others, thereby losing its authenticity as *faith*, dependent upon grace and revelation.

In this section we will look at the use Latin American theologians make of popular Jesus piety, and how it relates to the christologies they themselves propose. We will also consider the theological protests against the assumption that the meaning of Jesus and of discipleship is to be understood primarily or exclusively – or even perhaps at all – in terms of piety and the cult.

Four types of image of Christ have been distinguished in Latin American popular piety – the Subjugated Christ, the Dominant Christ, the Domesticated Christ and the Cultic Christ. We use the title Christ rather than the name Jesus here simply to indicate that none of these images involves much historical reference; or, more accurately, none lays much stress either on the humanity of Jesus or on the whole sweep of the narrative of the Jesus-event.

The Subjugated Christ is a wan, defeated, powerless figure. He is conquered, suffering and passive, the victim of a tragedy, resigned to his fate. Georges Casalis, the French Reformed theologian, describes this 'image of Jesus overcome, defeated' thus:

> In most instances he appears as one on the point of death – his eyes rolled up in their sockets, his face turned down to the earth, and his whole body exhibiting the havoc wrecked upon it by the blows of his torturers. All these representations arouse a morbid fascination. They reek of death . . . 'Our Abject Lord' this Christ is called. In Monserrat, near Bogota, atop a cliff overlooking the town, the Abject Lord has a sanctuary. Beneath the main altar, lying like Lenin in his mausoleum in Red Square, you can see his glass sepulchre. And suddenly you find yourself face to face with the bloodied visage of Jesus Defeated.
>
> (Bonino, 1984, p. 72)

And Casalis goes on to argue that in this image the poorest of the poor, the remaining Amerindians, subjugated for centuries, and the slum dwellers see themselves and their lot: 'It is their own destiny that they encounter here – and worship, and accept with masochistic resignation' (Bonino, 1984, p. 73). This image clearly encourages a culture of subjection and an attitude of passive acceptance.

A quite different figure is that of the Dominant Christ, the figure of Almighty God, triumphant, as the Great Conquistador. This, says Casalis, is God discarnate, the distant arbitrary God of omnipotence, not the Jesus who triumphed only on the Cross. This Christ appears with Mary at his side in Spanish regalia: 'Christ is represented as a celestial Ferdinand of Aragon, and Mary as an eternal Isabella of Castile' (Bonino, 1984, p. 74). Their pomp and power reflects that of the proud and oppressive colonialism of the past, but also legitimates and sanctifies the power structures of today.

The Domesticated Christ is a modern import, mainly from Protestant North America, but it has dovetailed with older types of devotion and influences Catholicism as well as Protestantism today. This Christ offers an individual salvation which provides for all our wants. he answers all our prayers, he consoles and comforts, but never challenges, disturbs or ventures to say anything at all about the public realm. If pressed, the preacher of this Christ will say that the problems of Latin America can only be solved by individuals turning to God; that is the first and last thing that a Christian has to say about politics. As a perceptive student commented on an evangelistic crusade in Costa Rica in 1972:

> This is a 'Father Christmas' Christ, one who comes to give only because he's so rich. He has lots of capital. Christ becomes a commodity, and the highest bidder gets him. All we hear is, 'Who wish to receive Christ as their personal Saviour, and not have to go to hell? Who wish to be healed this evening? Let's see the hands.' Those in need accept this gift of a witch-doctor Christ, and every time they see a minister it's 'Reverend, I hurt here,' or 'Reverend, please put your hand here and say a prayer.' The church starts looking like Jesus the Witch Doctor's hut. Jesus working cures? Sure he does, but cures aren't all there is – and they're certainly not supposed to be legal tender.
>
> (Bonino,1984, pp. 40–1)

This image is one that lives at peace with oppression and neo-colonialism. It has capitulated to the norms of the consumer society and become essentially materialist. It serves the function of inculcating in the poor the materialist values of the rich and of the exploiters. Of the three images of Christ we have discussed so far, this is the most remote from the Jesus of the gospels or the Good News of the Kingdom of God. There is little here of protest, or of the cry of the oppressed creature, no real care for neighbour to temper selfishness. Its main function is the internalization of the values of oppression.

The Cultic Christ, the figure at the centre of Christian worship, has also been distorted, Jon Sobrino and other Latin

American theologians argue, by being transformed into an omnipotent, triumphant Being whose Cross is seen as an exclusively *religious* event, the start of a great series of sacrificial rites. The Cross is no longer understood 'in all its unrepeatable and scandalous uniqueness', in its stark and terrible historicity, but as an instance, even the greatest instance, of the category of sacrifice as generally understood in religion. Believers relate to this Christ through worship, not through concrete discipleship of the historical Jesus, and in worship they believe that they have some kind of privileged access to him. There is then a tension, they assert, between cultic worship and discipleship; in worship it is only too easy to lose sight of the historical Jesus, of humanity in God, and of the call to struggle for humanity on earth (Sobrino, 1978, pp. 194, 275–7). This Christ, unlike the Jesus of the gospels, is remote from the ordinary people and their lot. In popular belief it is the saints and the Virgin who are the friends of the oppressed, who are already 'on their side', so that they may be approached with confidence for help. The Jesus whom they worship is seen as remote, powerful, requiring to be appeased and won over. In a quaint but significant inversion, an inscription in a church in Peru reads: 'Come to Mary, all ye who toil and are overburdened, and she will give you rest' (Bonino, 1984, p. 60). The saints are more accessible, welcoming and understanding than the Cultic Christ; folk turn to them as mediators and friends, and thereby confirm and strengthen the distortion in the image of Jesus which has had such harmful consequences for Christian faith.

Jesus, liberation theologians affirm, did not come to found a new religion but a new humanity. But amid all its distortions the Christian religion and the Christian cult preserve authentic possibilities of encounter with Jesus for the masses of the people.

KNOWING AND FOLLOWING JESUS

These different popular images of Jesus can only be adequately understood in the light of the social condition, the needs, fears and hopes, the history and the economic situation of those who find meaning in them. We have to ask why these particular people *need* such a figure of Jesus, what function this figure plays in their story, how it helps, or impedes, their way of relating to their world, how they understand their relationships and responsibilities.

The theologian may not analyse these images of Jesus and the implicit christologies that they represent from an olympian, objective standpoint. The theologian too is a social actor with a role and a place in a particular society; the theologian's judgement is profoundly conditioned by the fact that the theologian has interests, belongs to a class, has a recognized status and addresses a particular audience. These factors help the theologian to see some things and obscure others. The theologian cannot transcend social conditioning and take up a timeless, detached position, but it is possible, and important, to be as conscious as possible of the social influences on one's christological thinking. And this awareness should teach the theologian a proper modesty in the approach to popular images of Jesus, even if they seem primitive and superstitious. What simple people have made of Jesus is as much a datum for christology as the theologians' academic grappling with the tradition.

Both dogmatic christological definitions and popular images of Jesus are profoundly shaped by the culture, the needs and the interests of the age and of social groups. The only way to test these various understandings of Jesus in order to see if they are more than reflections of the spirit of the age, liberation theologians assert, is to compare them with the figure that emerges from the Gospel stories of Jesus. They are aware that it is no easy matter to discover the historical Jesus. The gospels witness to Jesus rather than describing, in a neutral way, what he did and who he was. But it is still important for a christology to be clearly in continuity with these earliest records and to centre on a Jesus who was a historical figure who trod the roads of Palestine in the early years of the Christian era. Otherwise, christology becomes no more than unrooted speculation about the nature of God, or the flowering of popular piety.

Why is there in liberation theology so strong an emphasis on the Jesus of history rather than the Jesus of popular devotion or the Christ of faith? Boff answers by suggesting that Latin Americans see strong similarities between their situation and that of Jesus' day and find Jesus' liberative programme and praxis compellingly attractive and relevant, as well as realistic in its recognition that liberation provokes conflict. The historical Jesus calls us to follow, and to meet him in the following which involves transforming this sinful world into the Kingdom of God. 'Jesus,' he writes, 'does not present himself as the explanation of reality. He presents himself as an urgent demand for the transformation of the reality . . . The historical Jesus represents a crisis, not a justification, for the world' (Boff, 1980, pp. 279–80). Abstract and speculative or popular and emotional images of Jesus are easily manipulated and distorted; as a corrective liberation theology seeks to rehabilitate the historical Jesus (Bonino, 1984, p. 167).

But it is quite specifically on the praxis of Jesus, rather than the teaching of Jesus, or teaching about Jesus, that attention is focused. The faith of Jesus, his relationships and attitudes to God and to people, his praying, his miracles, his passion and his resurrection are the nub of the matter. The teaching *of* Jesus illumines this, but must never be detached from it. And teaching *about* Jesus, as in the classic christological definitions, hardly engages at all with the praxis of Jesus, being concerned rather to clarify the relation of humanity and divinity within Jesus or the place of Jesus within the Trinity. Liberation theologians are not so naive as to suggest that the praxis of Jesus can be detached from all theological considerations, that here we have direct access to the historical reality of Jesus; but they argue that both the teaching of Jesus and teaching about Jesus are reflections upon what Jesus *does*, and the earliest strands of the tradition give a kind of primacy to the activity of Jesus. This must not be abandoned either in favour of liberalism's stress on Jesus as the the moral teacher *par excellence*, or traditional orthodoxy's tendency so to stress christological dogmas that the historicity and humanity of Jesus are obscured (Sobrino, 1978, pp. 374–81; Boff, 1980, pp. 122–38; Segundo, 1985, pp. 166–77).

Liberation christology stresses the humanity of Jesus, the One who is, in Boff's words, 'so radically human that he could only be God'. The divinity of Jesus is not to be sought apart from his humanity; it is in his humanity that God is present, in this humanity-that-is-divinity that God is made manifest. 'The incarnation therefore is not a confirmation of what we knew already. It communicates something new, even for God, and something that human beings did not know. Now human beings can live the event of the divine joyousness, by anticipation, inasmuch as it has become human in Jesus' (Bonino, 1984, pp. 24, 27).

In Jesus' praxis we see a manifestation, an authentic anticipation, of the kingdom of God, and simultaneously a new way opened by Jesus, the pioneer of faith. This is, in the fullest sense, 'liberation in process'. The miracles are signs of the presence of the Kingdom. Jesus' reaching out across social and cultural barriers, accepting all sorts of 'doubtful characters' and marginal people, and welcoming sinners and the despised to his table to eat with him, is liberating activity: 'He draws near to them because he is fleshing out in history the loving attitude of the Father towards the lowly and the sinful. Their present situation is not the last word on their life; it is not their final structure. They are not lost for good. God can liberate them' (Boff, 1980, p. 283).

In what sense, if any, may we see the praxis of Jesus as political – Jesus as a political figure? In the early days of liberation theology there were some who saw Jesus as a Zealot and were sympathetic to affirmations like 'For us Jesus Christ is Che Guevara' (Bonino, 1975, p. 2). But now there is the recognition that the Jesus of the Gospel stories was not a Zealot any more than he was a Saduccee or Essene, and that he cannot be labelled a political revolutionary in the conventional sense. Yet his message was the Good News of the Kingdom, and he was finally condemned for sedition. Accordingly, we may regard Jesus as a revolutionary in a qualified sense, being careful to distinguish his revolution from the limited, nationalist or purely this-worldly revolutions espoused by others. Clodovis Boff puts it thus:

> Jesus was not, historically, a militant in the strict political sense, understanding politics as the superstructure encasing every-

thing else, invested with the exercise of authority over the whole
of society. He did not strive to do away with all authority, after
the manner of an anarchist, or to inaugurate a new authority in a
rough and brutal manner. Rather he accepted established authority critically – *juxta modum*, with reservations, only so far. On
the other hand, if we take the word 'revolution' in its broader
acceptation, as denoting any radical change or structural transformation, then we would have to say that Jesus was revolutionary, and more than revolutionary, for the radicalism of his
message and example can transform human beings and conse-
quently their social structures – can translate itself into social
action. In this sense we could say that Jesus was the greatest
revolutionary in the history of civilization.

(Bonino,1975, p. 18)

This Jesus stood, and stands, as a sign of 'contradiction' in the
midst of a world that is full of contradictions and conflicts. As
Segundo argues in meticulous detail, Jesus agitated the political scene in Israel but cannot be labelled a political agitator; he
sought out and sharpened the main conflicts in Israelite society.
'The mere proclamation of the proximity of the kingdom, as
something that will bring blessedness to the poor and woe to the
rich, not only points up the opposing situation of the two groups
in Israel but also undermines the very foundations of the peace-
ful co-existence that had been typical between them' (Segundo,
1985, p. 76). The established authorities responded to Jesus and
his movement with violence and the execution of an innocent
man because they saw him as interfering in their sphere and as a
threat to their power and to the existing order. Can one really
affirm that this was a misunderstanding on their part? But, on
the other hand, the issues raised by Jesus are so profound and
ultimate and the conflict he arouses so fundamental to the
human condition that he cannot be recruited into any party, programme or ideology. He never sought political power for himself
or aligned his movement with any of the social or political
options of the day. His revolution was in the depths, but caused
disturbance at every level. And this it continues to do today.

Along with this stress on the praxis of the historical Jesus as
the criterion for all theology and devotion, liberation theologians stress that knowing Jesus and commitment to him are

inseparable. Detached, 'objective' knowledge of Jesus is no more than fragmentary; true theology involves commitment. Thus it is a question of following as a disciple in the company of disciples the way of the historical Jesus and participating in the praxis of the Kingdom he proclaimed. Only so can we come to know Jesus as the one who brings close the Kingdom of God rather than a Jesus who is a construction of our minds, a projection of our desires and fears.

Following Jesus is the way to knowing Jesus as the Christ. This following, unlike devotion to an idol we have made for ourselves, involves conversion, a radical change of direction: 'We can come to know Jesus as the Christ,' writes Sobrino, 'only insofar as we start a new life, break with the past and undergo conversion, engage in Christian practice and fight for the justice of God's kingdom' (Sobrino, 1978, p. xxiv). This is a radical conversion, not simply a change of mind or of attitude, but a reorientation of the whole person and immersion in a new praxis. And the conversion of the person in fellowship with others goes along with the transformation of the world. Christology accordingly is not concerned in isolation with the explication of the significance of Jesus of Nazareth, but is inextricably involved with the transformation of people, societies and the world. Concrete disicpleship means involvement in the transformation of the world, in the seeking of the Kingdom of God and his righteousness.

There is thus no apolitical christology. As Boff writes:

> No christology is or can be neutral. Every christology is partisan and committed. Willingly or unwillingly christological discourse is voiced in a given social setting with all the conflicting interests that pervade it. That holds true as well for theological discourse that claims to be 'purely' theological, historical, traditional, ecclesial and apolitical. Normally such discourse adopts the position of those who hold power in the existing system. If a different kind of christology with its own commitments appears on the scene and confronts the older 'apolitical' christology, the latter will soon discover its social locale, forget its 'apolitical' nature, and reveal itself as a religious reinforcement of the existing status quo.
>
> (Boff, 1980, pp. 265-6)

The problem here is that if one suggests, as Boff does, that *the* function of christology 'is to shape and work out a Christian option in society' (Boff, 1980, p. 293), there is no safeguard left against christology becoming simply a manifesto, a political programme or an ideological weapon. But truth claims must not be disregarded. Liberation theologians affirms that serious engagement with the truth of christology is inseparable from political commitment, not that christology can be reduced to exclusively political or practical dimensions.

'Is the Christ-event "exhausted" ', asks J. Severino Croatto, 'or is it a reservoir of meaning for the deed of liberation to which, for example, our dominated Latin America aspires?' (Bonino, 1984, p. 112). Latin American Christians emphatically find in Jesus Christ a perennial source of meaning and motivation, and are producing christological reflection which is clearly not an ideology of liberation with christological decoration, but a serious grappling with the enduring issues and the recovery of virtually forgotten themes and emphases.

CHAPTER 6

The Church, Theology and the Poor

Theology and sociology provide rather different accounts of the Church. Their method and conclusions are so distinct that an outside observer might suppose that they were examining quite different phenomena – which, in a sense, is true. It is rare to find any integration of the two accounts, or any serious attempt to come to terms with their discrepancies and press forward to a more rounded way of understanding. It is one of the contributions of liberation theology today to press for this more comprehensive approach, in which theological analysis relates to empirical realities, and sociological conclusions provide the matter for theological reflection.

Ecclesiology, that subsection of theology which concerns itself specifically with the Church, understands the Church in terms of its foundation and destiny, its calling and its role in the economy of salvation, what the Church is there for, and what part it plays in God's purposes. The classic images of the Church – the Body of Christ, the Bride of Christ, the household of faith, the pilgrim people of God, and so on – are enrolled as symbols of the perennial essence of the Church, timeless pointers to an unchanging reality rather than traditional symbols to be creatively applied in new situations. It is the same with the standard lists of the 'marks' of the Church – oneness, holiness, catholicity and apostolicity – which are treated as the criteria through which one may discern the existence of a Church which is the same always, and everywhere and for everyone. More modern emphases – on the Church as the sacrament of the unity of all humankind, or as the sign and anticipation of the Kingdom, for example – show a similar concern with the universal and the ideal, and impatience with particularities and specifics. And when the fact that the Church is a human institution is taken seriously, there is a tendency to absolutize a particular shape and structure of the Church. Church structures become part of the revelation, part of the 'given' of faith, things that cannot be changed and must be the same everywhere and always. And even as significant a move from a juridical and institutional understanding of the Church towards making the image of 'the pilgrim people of God' dominant as that effected by the Second Vatican Council, for all its positive impact, still leaves us with an abstract, general notion of 'people', unrelated to class, culture or history.

Even the best, most forward-looking recent ecclesiology, such as Hans Küng's notable book *The Church* (English Trans. 1968), does not escape this charge. No account is taken here of sociological insights or of the diverse empirical realities of the life of the Church today. The Church is presented as a kind of implant from above into a particular society which transcends all cultures and classes and is not implicated in social structures or caught up in compromises with social power. This kind of Church sees itself as always and everywhere occupying a higher ground from which it may address society with authority.

The sociological approach is particularly indebted to the thought of Emile Durkheim (1858–1917) and Max Weber (1864–1920). It starts from the assumption that the Church is one social institution among others, which can be adequately understood with little, if any, reference to its own self-understanding, i.e. to theology. As one of a class of institutions vital for the well-being of society, the Church performs, well or badly, a range of important social functions. The sociologist sees clearly what the theologian tends to neglect: that the Church is deeply implicated in the class, power and economic structures of a particular society. Willy-nilly the Church is involved in social conflict, much of its behaviour and indeed its theology can only be understood in the light of its own social composition, and much of its structure and organization reflects the social order in which it is set. Its functions include

the provision of 'social cement', the legitimation of authority
and the confirmation of the social structure. It is not easy for it
to transcend its social setting or escape from its social
determinants.

The attempt to hold these two approaches together and assert
that they provide us with distinct but complementary truths
has never been easy or common. Yet this is precisely what any
serious political theology should attempt – *both* to grasp the
enduring God-given reality and calling of the Church *and* to
explore the specific ways in which this reality relates to
particular societies, economies and power structures in specific
times and places; to grasp the constraints and opportunities
which specific situations present for the Church; and to
compare the functions the Church actually fulfils in one context
with those it ought to fulfil. Ecclesiology cannot be simply the
ideology of the Church as it is today, defending, explaining and
justifying matters as they are, expounding but not questioning
the teaching of the Church and supporting uncritically Church
structures. For theology is concerned with the Kingdom, of
which the Church is called to be a sign and a foretaste; and with
the Church's Lord, to whom the Church is often disobedient;
and with the world, of which Jesus is also Lord, the world God
loved so much that he sent his Son. The world in which the
Church exists is full of conflicts and divisions; society is divided
into classes, races, genders and so forth. Only too often, as in
Northern Ireland, the Church in her divisions mirrors, confirms
and exacerbates the divisions of society. Theology is well
advised to be realistic in its analysis of what actually happens in
the Church and in the world, and rigorous in its attempt to
discern the vocation of the Church, for *this* is the Church that is
called to prefigure the Kingdom, and *this* is the world for which
Christ died. A theology of the Church which never attends to
the constraints and opportunities involved in the fact that the
Church is a social institution is at least as unhelpful and
defective as a sociology of the Church which never gets beyond
institutional analysis to ask what the Church is *for*.

Liberation theology sees itself as more a 'Church theology'
than most other contemporary theology. Its task is a service of
the Church, and on behalf of the Church to the world. The life

and activity of the Church are regarded as major subjects for theological reflection, and liberation theologians see themselves as responsible to the Church. The theologian is the friendly critic of the Church, and theological work is done in critical solidarity with the Church. In close alliance with the social scientists, the theologian examines the actuality of the Church in relation to society. And, not surprisingly, a good proportion of the better-known liberation theologians have dual academic qualifications – in theology and in a social science.

But of what 'church' does liberation theology see itself as the servant? It certainly does not relate to some timeless ideal notion of the Church, an 'invisible Church' which has no empirical manifestation in history. Nor does it see theology as the servant of the hierarchy, or the mouthpiece of the teaching magisterium. Rather, liberation theology is rooted in the Church as people, and people in a quite concrete sense – people who belong to classes, people involved in social conflicts and, because it is the *Christian* Church, especially people who are poor, powerless and oppressed.

Liberation theology arose as a response to outrageous poverty, injustice and oppression and as a protest against the inadequacy of the institutional Church's engagement with these issues. But its specific roots are in the emergence of the so-called 'base communities' in many countries of Latin America. Accordingly, we have to turn to some apparently rather narrow domestic problems in the Latin American churches if we are to understand the roots of liberation ecclesiology. A variety of quite specific challenges were being posed to the Latin American churches long before the Second Vatican Council. But not until the Council was it possible to discuss these openly and freely. And it was not just abstract theological questions which arose: the base communities raised questions, and also provided experiments, in different ways of being the Church.

BASE COMMUNITIES IN LATIN AMERICA

Base Christian communities arose largely spontaneously in many countries of Latin America, but particularly in Brazil, in the 1950s and 1960s as imaginative responses to a series of crises and challenges in the Church.

An increasingly severe shortage of vocations meant that many vast parishes could not regularly have the services of a priest and were accordingly deprived of the Mass for long periods. The hierarchies responded in various ways. Lay pastoral workers were recruited in increasing numbers. In some areas villages without priests were issued with radios so that they could follow Mass broadcast from the cathedral. In a poverty-stricken area of Brazil there were some 1400 'radio communities' by the mid-1960s (Cox, 1984, p. 113). The Vatican, alarmed at the predicament of the Latin American churches, encouraged a 'Mission to Latin America' on the part of the US Catholic Church, which in the 1960s despatched large numbers of priests and religious. The intention was to strengthen the traditional structure and operation of the Latin American churches; it was essentially a conservative under-standing of the Church and its role in society that underlay the project. The effect was unexpected: many of the missionaries were quickly radicalized by their encounter with poverty and degradation, and began to question power structures in Church and society which caused or tolerated such obscenities. Back in the United States the missionaries stimulated an uneasy conscience about economic and political relationships with the nations to the south. The Vatican and most of the Latin American hierarchies had for some time been disturbed by the spread of socialist ideas and the appeal of socialism. But the Mission ironically helped to ensure that socialist ideas were taken increasingly seriously within the churches in Latin America, and the Christian acceptability of capitalism more vigorously questioned at home.

The appeal of Protestantism was also a problem that the Mission was intended to help to solve. Protestant congre-gations were usually much smaller than the vast and often impersonal Catholic parishes, and their worship and organ-ization more relaxed and informal, with the laity playing a major role. Parishes which languished without a priest often saw their neighbouring Protestant congregations flourishing and growing. This shortage of priests stimulated and enabled a range of experiments into what it means to be the Church, and this experience in its turn sparked off much fundamental reconsideration of the theology of Church and ministry on the part of theologians such as Leonardo Boff and Jon Sobrino. For many, the experience of the base communities amounted to a rediscovery of the Church.

The Second Vatican Council had attempted, with limited success, to play down the juridical and institutional understanding of the Church in favour of seeing the Church as the people of God, a fellowship rather than a power structure. Pope John XXIII had gone further, and spoken of his hopes that the Council might make the Church 'the Church of all the people and, in particular, of the poor' (In Cox, 1984, p. 110). The endeavour was to counterbalance the traditional emphasis on the hierarchical nature of the Church with a new stress on the Church as a pilgrim fellowship of people. Sobrino saw this as 'a step in the direction of what might be called a theological democratization of the Church' (Sobrino, 1985, p. 92). But it was not a definitive and irreversible move which demanded a radical reconsideration of the older hierarchical ecclesiology. The Second Vatican Council in fact declared that hierarchy was necessary for the proper functioning and true being of the Church. And some people assumed that this implied a justification of the centralization of power in society as well. The Council certainly made some use of the rhetoric of 'a preferential option for the poor' and the 'church of the poor', but did not allow these concepts to affect its basic ecclesiology or its proposals for the reform and renewal of the Church (Chenu, 1977; Sobrino, 1985, pp. 91, 134). 'The poor' was never used in a concrete or specific way and hence the challenge to the Church was understood very generally. But, for all that, the Council stimulated an openness to innovation and experiment which was made full use of in many places. For example, it encouraged the repossession of the Bible by the people which was discussed in chapter 4. All this gave a degree of recognition and support to the base communities, and they spread rapidly in the 1960s and early 1970s.

Base Christian communities, or the Iglesia Popular, the people's church, are fellowships of the poor which have emerged mainly in the urban slums of Latin America. They understand themselves as the Church at the foot of the pile, the Christian fellowships at the base of the social pyramid. As such, they believe that they are rediscovering something of the authenticity of what it means to be the Church. Their structure varies, but it is always characterized by an emphasis on lay leadership and a search for consensus in decision-making: it is the community that takes decisions, that gathers around the Word, that discerns and responds to the call of God. Their worship is informal and open, in a way that more structured and authoritarian worship is not, to the expression and celebration of the varied gifts of the members of the community. And they are deeply involved in the popular movement for liberation. Base Christian communities are politically engaged; they see themselves as having a clear and unavoidable role in the political struggle: 'The Basic Ecclesial Communities participate in the liberation movements and, within these, create a dimension within which Christians can pray, celebrate their faith and read the Bible. Thus, Basic Ecclesial Communities become a focus for liberating evangelization and for teaching the faith to the people within the very core of the liberation movement' (Richard, 1984, p. 11). They are churches *of* the poor, rather than middle-class churches which speak *for* the poor. They do not see themselves as an anti-Church, a para-Church or a sect; they, along with others, *are* the Church.

The development of base communities is, Leonardo Boff suggests, a true *ecclesiogenesis*, the emergence of a new form and a new understanding of the Church. This is nevertheless a repossession of ancient forms and fully in continuity with the tradition: 'a new church, but not one that is different from the church of the apostles and the tradition' (In Torres and Eagleson, 1981, p. 133). It appears first at the margins of society and challenges the power structures at the heart, both of the institutional Church and the economic/political order. At the periphery, in the slums around the great cities, a new freedom and creativity have been found, and opportunities for 'a pure and evangelical simplicity'. Boff is not surprised that there is tension between this 'new church' and the 'old church'. For him the base communities exist for the renewal, revitalization and reform rather than replacement of the institutional

Church. But he is aware of the tensions: there is constant suspicion that the base communities are becoming a para-Church, fundamentally opposed to the institutional Church and showing heretical and sectarian tendencies. They must not be intimidated by such suspicions:

> The new church will have to remain faithful to its path. It will have to be loyally disobedient. It will have to seek a profound loyalty to the demands of the gospels. Critically reflecting upon these questions and convinced of its path, it must have the courage to be disobedient to the demands of the centre, without anger or complaint, in deep adherence to the desire to be faithful to the Lord, the gospels, and the Spirit – the same desire that is presumed to motivate the institutional church.
>
> (Boff, 1985, p. 63)

The function of the Church, for Boff, is to 'make visible and historical the salvific efficacy of Jesus Christ and his mission', to be the 'sacrament-sign' and 'sacrament-instrument' of liberation, to give the Gospel 'concrete historical embodiment in the midst of social reality' (in Torres and Eagleson, 1987, p. 125). And as soon as we face the issue of the concrete historical embodiment of the Church we have to face the question of how the Church exists within a class society, since our societies are divided into classes. There are, Boff suggests, two dimensions to the Church. It is a complex ecclesiastical institution, and it is 'a sacrament, sign and instrument of salvation'. The two need to be held together, for 'the institution is the vehicle for the sacrament. The social visibility of the church makes palpable the grace and kingdom of God' (in Torres and Eagleson, 1981, p. 126). Accordingly, when we are examining the institutional Church we have to ask how effectively it makes the grace and Kingdom of God palpable, how suitable its structures are as a sacramental vehicle. The class society in which the Latin America Church is implicated is one in which the various classes have conflicting interests, in which there is a high degree of inequality and in which some classes dominate and oppress the others. Class structure profoundly influences the whole of life, so that people construe reality in terms of their class position and interests.

The Church is not immune to the tensions of society. It is, Boff says, 'inevitably riddled with class conflicts' (in Torres and Eagleson, 1981, p. 129). The ruling classes expect the Church to legitimate and support their dominance. But the oppressed classes also appeal to the Church to support their struggle. And the Church's response is conditioned by its history, by the stances it has taken in the past and by the social alliances which it has forged. Boff believes that the institutional Church has come more and more to reflect in its organization and policies its long-term liaison with the powerful classes. Thus he argues that in the beginnings of the Church the people participated in decision-making and power was shared. Gradually, however, the people have been marginalized and power has been concentrated in the hands of a small elite of 'experts and hierarchical officials'. The people, the vast majority of the Church, became dependent on the hierarchy; the rights and responsibilities they once had were now expropriated. And, in thus reflecting the power structure of society, the Church was understood as legitimating it. Today, there is a fundamental tension within the institutional Church – on the one hand, it is deeply implicated in capitalist society and gives it its implied or explicit support; on the other hand, it is the sign and instrument of the Kingdom, witnessing to a very different kind of society.

The institutional Church, Boff argues, is not inescapably locked into either possibility. Historically, in Latin America there has been a particularly close alliance between the Church and the dominant classes. But the base communities and liberation theology are challenging this and embodying the other possibility of being the Church. A Church linked to the dominant class develops a theology and an ecclesiology appropriate to this alliance. The oneness of the Church is seen as monolithic uniformity with a strong centralization of power as the indispensable way of maintaining unity. Holiness is interpreted as obedience to the ecclesiastical system. Few modern saints, Boff argues, are lay people, almost all are ecclesiastics of one kind or another, 'saints of the system'. Prophets, reformers, critics are not regarded as saints, but as deviants to be disciplined into conformity. Apostolicity is a quality of the holders of offices which they have received through 'apostolic succession', not of the whole people of God. Catholicity means institutional and liturgical unity across cultures – the same hierarchy, the same sacraments, the same theology everywhere. Such a Church, Boff suggests, is not an effective vehicle for the message and the praxis of Jesus. Its internal contradictions are so sharp that there must be a radical reform, a thorough restructuring of the Church so that it may be more faithful to its calling and more capable of carrying out its task.

The Marxists are wrong in saying that the Church is essentially conservative. Since at its heart is 'the dangerous and subversive memory of Jesus of Nazareth, who was crucified under Pontius Pilate', it is inherently revolutionary. In certain social situations, and provided it has an eye to the Christian integrity of its own structures and modes of operation, the Church can perform a revolutionary function and stand with the oppressed in their struggle. This is particularly possible in Latin America where the worldview of the common people is predominantly religious, and the majority regard themselves as members of the Church. It is in this light that we can understand the emergence of the grass-roots Church, the base communities, a Church linked to the subordinate classes (in Torres and Eagleson, 1981, pp. 124–32).

Boff argues that in the base communities the oppressed and excluded people become the people of God, 'communities of baptized people, communities of faith, hope, and love that are animated by Jesus Christ's message of absolute fraternity, and propose to flesh out in the concrete a people made up of free, communal, participant human beings. This . . . signifies an anticipation of, and a preparation for, the Kingdom of God and God's eschatological people' (in Torres and Eagleson, 1981, p. 134). Because they are committed both to the Gospel and to political action, because they are so critical of the institutional Church and of oppressive social, political and economic structures and relationships, it is not surprising that base communities have often been regarded with suspicion and frequently attacked. But they have their support as well, above all when the bishops, gathered at the Conference of the Latin American Hierarchies in Pueblo, declared them to be 'a reason for joy and hope for the church'.

'The poor', wrote Gustavo Gutierrez, 'raise the question of what "being the church" really means' (Guiterrez, 1977, p. 11). Is a Church in which the poor do not belong truly the Church of Jesus Christ? If one accepts in full seriousness the patristic adage, *ubi Christus ibi ecclesia* (where Christ is, there is the Church), surely we must discover among the poor both the Christ who chooses to identify with them and the true nature of the Church. The concept of the Church as a perfect society, powerful and wealthy, parallel to the state and able to pontificate to the state, has few attractions for the poor even if it claims to speak on their behalf. For its is not *their* Church; they do not belong to it, except as dependents. In such a Church, as in the broader society, they are powerless and excluded. In important senses, this Church and class society are mirror images of one another; the place of the poor is the same in each, although the Church may be more benevolent in its attitudes and dealings. What it will not do is set aside its institutional arrogance and attend to the poor, listen to what they have to say and welcome the gifts and insights that they bring. Nor will it risk taking a stand on their side, challenging oppression head-on, or sacrifice its own wealth, security or standing.

The poor therefore challenge the power structures of the Church and the centralization of authority in the hierarchy, together with the Church's implication in class society despite its claim to transcend the social and political order. The challenge is intended to renew and reform rather than destroy the Church. Sobrino suggests that the poor may be the resurrection of the true Church; through the poor whom he loves Jesus Christ is recreating the entire Church (Sobrino, 1985, p. 93). Yet the poor are a constant irritant to a complacent and triumphalist understanding of the Church; their presence makes reality unavoidable. Their claim and their condition keep alive the questions of God and of the Kingdom and ensure that the Church cannot be finally domesticated within the power structures of society. The poor bring to the Church an understanding of fellowship, sharing, solidarity, which is a reminder that an important dimension of catholicity is the sharing of one another's burdens. They see the Church not so much as a mechanism for conservation and legitimation, but as a fellowship which is an agency of change. In the Church of the poor, and through the Church of the poor, the people of God take their share in human liberation. And, inevitably, this involves the Church, as well as individual Christians, in taking sides, in conflict.

Liberation theology is 'Church theology' in a precise and rather unusual sense. It arises out of a specific Church experience – that of the base communities – and liberation theologians recognize that on the basis of this experience they have a particular responsibility to the whole Church. They allow the base communities to set the agenda for theology, and they try to articulate and interpret the significance of this new experience of what it means to be the Church. This is not 'theology from above', whether that means pronouncements handed down by the magisterium or learned tomes dealing with questions asked only by other theologians. It acts as a mouth-piece for the poor and the oppressed. It speaks from within the fray, not from a secure standpoint above the conflict; it cannot avoid taking sides. Thus theology and social criticism are inseparable, and together provide an interpretation of social conflict as seen from below.

Base communities do not, however, spontaneously generate coherent theology. They provide stimulus, insights and material for theological reflection rather than a ready-made theology. They insist that 'theology is too important to be left to the theologians'; ordinary folk have as important a contribution to make as scholars. Liberation theologians claim that they do not idealize or sacralize the poor, but they also refuse to believe that academics or Church leaders who distance themselves from the experience of the grass-roots communities are capable of developing an adequate theology. 'Experts' should be viewed with some suspicion, especially when they discount the significance of the opinions and practice of ordinary people.

THE BOURGEOIS CAPTIVITY OF THE NORTHERN CHURCHES

The churches in the northern hemisphere exist in a radically different social, economic and political context. The societies in

which they are set are very much more prosperous than the
countries of Latin America. They have their poor, it is true,
but the poor are not the majority of the population, as in
Latin America, and the poverty of the North, serious as it is,
cannot be compared with the destitution of the slums and
shanty towns of the South. Class conflicts exist in the North
but, for a variety of reasons, they are not as blatant and
savage as in the South. Northern societies are more secular
and more pluralistic. The majority are democracies with
much less blatant and obvious oppression on the part of the
police and the military.

Most churches in the northern hemisphere have for a long
time been in a process of remorseless decline in numbers and in
influence. Only in isolated pockets here and there can any
church claim to be 'the church of the people'. The majority do
not belong to any church and take little part in religious
activities, save perhaps for a few rites of passage – baptisms,
marriages and funerals – and some christianized folk festivals.
Although there is still a widespread acceptance of what may in
some sense be termed Christian values, although the clergy are
in general well thought of, and although many more people than
appear on the churches' books have some vague but significant
sense of belonging, it is no longer possible to speak of even the
larger denominations as 'churches of the people'. Worldviews
do not appear to be very significantly influenced by the
Christian faith, only a minority regard themselves as members
of any church, and levels of participation in church activities are
low and continue to fall sharply, particularly among young
people. There are exceptions, of course. In Poland and Ireland
the Roman Catholic Church is very much the church of the
people. The United States has periodic booms in religious
observance but here, as elsewhere, the diversity of denominations makes it impossible to speak of a church of the
people.

Today's ecclesiastical fragmentation seems to be the religious
reflex of a pluralistic society. Religion becomes another area of
free consumer choice, and churches understand themselves as
competing with one another to get a larger share of the market.
Denominations frequently and unconsciously come to represent

class or ethnic groups, reflecting and reinforcing the existing distinctions in the community. Even efforts towards a wider Christian unity are often understood on the analogy of mergers or take-overs in the business world. In all this, it becomes increasingly difficult to see anywhere the church of the people.

Even in their depleted state, the churches of the North tend to cling onto the vestiges of their old alliance with wealth and power. Senior ecclesiastics act as chaplains or confessors to the powerful. Elite education, as in the English private schools, is powerfully influenced by the established Church. The armed forces employ chaplains. In some countries the state levies a church tax and pays clergy; in a few the state continues to have influence over top ecclesiastical appointments and the Church is represented in the legislature or has other ways of influencing government directly. In the United States, despite the constitutional separation of Church and state, there is (as Will Herberg showed) an implicit 'establishment' of religion as such, rather than of any one denomination (Herberg, 1960). And with the rise of the New Christian Right, it is clear that organized religious groups can still have considerable influence on the political process. These linkages with power are not just odd anachronisms; they can all be used in a responsible and Christian way. We mention them here very briefly because they symbolize 'a church linked to the dominant class', to use Boff's phrase; and because the Church has been much more successful, for whatever reason, in maintaining and sometimes strengthening them than it has been in sustaining its links with the poor.

There are hardly any churches *of* the poor in the northern hemisphere. The nearest equivalents are not really *churches*, in the sociological sense, but small pentecostalist *sects* among ethnic minorities, or some of the black churches in the USA, or storefront congregations in the urban slums. It is broadly true that in Europe the churches have never really incorporated the working classes since the Industrial Revolution. In more recent times it has become clear that church decline takes place at a far faster pace among the poor, so that the churches which remain in working-class housing schemes and inner-city slums have pitifully low levels of attendance. They tend to be regarded as missions of a middle-class church *to* the poor rather than, as in any real sense, churches *of* the poor. Sometimes they operate as escalators out of poverty for the fortunate few, escape hatches out of deprivation, rather than churches of and for the poor. Their position is often strangely anomalous, standing both for Christianity and for middle-class values, and hardly aware that there may be a tension between the two. Thus, poor people often regard them as implants which demonstrate the ominous syncretism between Christianity and the values of bourgeois capitalist society which Lesslie Newbigin discerns in the affluent North.

This type of syncretism is only possible for a private version of Christian faith which sees religion as addressing itself for the most part to issues of private morality and domestic affairs. It is reluctant to confront head-on the prevailing values and mores of capitalist society, and in the United States, where church-going is at a far higher level than in Europe (though, here too, the poor are less likely to be practising Christians) articulate sections of the Church proclaim that there is an organic link between Christianity and free-market capitalism. In such a situation the poor, the victims of the system, are marginalized. And if they inhale the prevailing ideology, they internalize the very values which deny their worth, so that the victims blame themselves for their condition.

Post-Christendom churches represent minorities which no longer have a recognized right to influence power. They are more likely to reflect rather than shape values and policies. They tend to use the remaining fragments of their former influence to defend the institutional interests of the Church. Beyond that, they may issue broad hortatory generalizations on the issues of the day, which are not expected even by those who produce them to affect significantly subsequent events. The Church understands itself as standing above the political struggle and viewing it from on high.

Political theology generated in such a context tends to be 'from above' – Church leaders and professional theologians speaking on behalf of the institutional Church to the powerful and the decision-makers. In this dialogue of elites, the shared assumption is that the Church is still a significant part of the power structure of society, and that theology has the capacity to resolve, or assist in resolving, the problems of 'the world'. Because it is directed at the decision-makers, such theology usually shows much sympathy and understanding for the problems that they face and great confidence in their basic integrity and prudence. The dilemmas of the powerful rather than the problems of the poor are the primary concern. The Christendom model of the relationship of Church and society lingers on as Church leaders and theologians show themselves very aware of pastoral responsibilities towards the powerful, and very nervous about taking sides in a way which might disturb their access to the corridors of power. The hierarchy speaks for a Church which is believed to transcend social divisions and which must be kept united at almost any cost. And the statements that emerge are usually bland and general; they do not confront 'the powers' or challenge the existing order. The role of the Church is understood as the laying down of principles, usually of so general an order as to be uncontroversial. Implementation, policy choices and the taking of sides are matters best left to the individual. And from this whole process of theologizing the poor are effectively excluded.

Three factors in the present situation of the churches in the North give us ground for hope when we contemplate this bourgeois captivity. First, the Church is still *there*, with the poor. However weak and distorted its presence, however insignificant may be its numbers, the Church is still visibly present in the urban slums and the peripheral housing estates. And, at least in some situations, it is listening and learning, and finding in its weakness that it is in solidarity with the marginalized. Secondly, even a frail and compromised Church still has the Gospel. The disturbing memory of Jesus Christ calls it to renewal, to a rediscovery of what it is to be the Church, to a determination to transcent social determinants and break free from easy compromises with the values of the consumer society. Thirdly, in its new-found weakness, the Church has the opportunity to rediscover what it means to be a creative minority, the salt of the earth, the leaven of the lump. The post-Constantinian era may be the time when a pre-Constantinian understanding of the Church can be recovered. A minority Church which is no longer a major social institution or a recognized part of political society may well be a Church that is set free from many social restraints, enabling it to *be* the Church.

And, indeed, there are a number of encouraging, and largely unexpected, developments among the churches of the North which may give hope for the future. The picture is not simply one of decline, decay and demoralization. There are some signs of a new, questioning, critical and prophetic theology emerging in frail and fragmentary form alongside the more established and recognized academic and ecclesiastical styles of theology which have been dominant for so long. These developments are rooted in certain forms of Christian response to some contemporary crises, of which three deserve particular mention: the crisis of *legitimacy*, the crisis of *institutions* and the crisis of *community*.

There is, first, a crisis of legitimacy. In their very different fashions, Jürgen Habermas (1976, 1981) and Alastair MacIntyre (1981) have analysed the breakdown of the traditional forms of legitimating authority in the modern world. MacIntyre sees the problem as essentially an intellectual crisis: no longer is there a generally accepted criterion by reference to which value conflicts may be resolved and the social system validated. For Habermas, in late capitalist society, the inherited forms of legitimation which veiled and made acceptable class domination have been dissolved away, leaving the system without the necessary means of eliciting loyalty.

At a more impressionistic level, it seems clear that during the post-war decades of the Keynesian consensus (which was also the period of the 'secular' theologies) acute problems of legitimacy did not commonly arise in most of the countries of the North. There was a comparatively strong cross-party agreement about values and goals which seemed to make religious legitimation superfluous. Intelligent people confidently proclaimed 'the end of ideology' and seemed to believe that religious dogma, like secular philosophies and systems of ideas, had permanently withdrawn from a public realm which would now conduct its affairs on a 'rational' or pragmatic basis without reference to religious or metaphysical matters. With the emergence as a major political force of the New Right in the 1970s the consensus was shattered and the new politics was unashamedly doctrinaire. Mr Reagan declared himself a born-again Christian and was hoisted to power with the support of the Moral Majority and the evangelical stars of the electronic church. Mrs Thatcher pronounced St Francis's prayer (Lord, make me an instrument of your peace) on the steps of No. 10 Downing Street before entering for the first time as Prime Minister, and has shown herself far more interested in Church affairs than most of her predecessors for many years. The Right in general claims Church legitimation, and is amazed and angry when it does not receive it – as has happened increasingly, particularly in Britain. Not only does the Right believe that it is entitled to such support, but it seems to feel that religion is the necessary grounding for its policies and its regimes. Events like the service to mark the end of the Falklands war, when Church leaders refused to allow a triumphant celebration of victory, arouse rage in high places, while repeated questioning of key government policies in areas as varied as poverty, race relations and nuclear deterrence provokes outbursts of petulance or anger from ministers. All this, together with some reflective writing by thinkers like Roger Scruton and Maurice Cowling, suggests that there is a new awareness on the Right of the need for religious legitimation. Meanwhile, the Left welcome the interventions of the Church whenever they seem sympathetic to its policies, but does not commonly allocate a recognized place in its scheme of things for the Church and for theology. It welcomes the Church as an ally, but does not often look for religious legitimation (Turner, 1983, pp. 178–98).

Secondly, there is a crisis of institutions. This is to be understood in large part as the structural reflex of the crisis of legitimacy. For a significant section of the population, the old loyalties to trade unions and political parties are not as firm as once they were, the parliamentary process is not treated with such respect, and the police are not seen as impartial. Trust in major social institutions is markedly eroded, and large groups like the unemployed, ethnic minorities or striking coalminers feel themselves marginalized and forgotten. No one of significance, they often feel, really listens to them, their voice is not heard. During the Coal Strike in Britain in 1984 to whom did such people turn? Surprisingly, often they went to the vicar or to the bishop. And, quite unexpectedly, the Church became a spokesman for the dumb, with David Jenkins and others denouncing government and union and calling on people to find hope by facing up to 'what is going on, what is wrong in it, and what might be brought out of it'. Similarly, in the inner-city problems of the great conurbations, as in Liverpool, it has been the Church leaders who have been pushed into prominence, almost despite themselves. And by default – because few other people are really looking the problems in the eye – it has been the churches that have had to address the problem of the decay of the cities in notable productions such as the Report of the Archbishop's Commission on Urban Priority Areas, *Faith in the City* (1985), which was denounced by leading Conservative politicians before publication as a Marxist document! We should not pretend that the Church is unaffected by the crisis of institutions. It is at least as deeply involved as any other major social institution – perhaps more so. But the Church does seem to have some capacity to rise to the occasion and recover something of its true vocation, even in the countries of the North in the 1980s.

In the third place, there is a crisis of community, a breakdown of fellowship. In such a situation each congregation of the Church is capable of being an experiment in what community means, a rediscovery of fellowship. The base communities of Latin America are just this. In a context where structures of oppression have eroded fellowship to a disastrous extent and where the institutional Church is often too cumbersome, vast and self-concerned to manifest community, the base communities have reinvented Christian fellowship, and seen their experience of community as a clue to what the broader society might, and must, become. Alastair MacIntyre concludes his remarkable book, *After Virtue*, with a response to the contemporary crisis of community. He draws an analogy with the decline of the Roman empire and the start of the Dark Ages, when men and women of good will ceased to identify the continuance of civility and moral community with the maintenance of the Roman *imperium*:

What they set themselves to achieve instead – often not recognizing fully what they were doing – was the construction of new forms of community within which the moral life could be sustained so that both morality and civility might survive the coming ages of barbarism and darkness . . . For some time now we too have reached that turning point. What matters at this stage is the construction of local forms of community within which civility and the intellectual and moral life can be sustained through the new dark ages that are already upon us. And if the tradition of the virtues was able to survive the horrors of the last dark ages, we are not entirely without grounds for hope. This time, however, the barbarians are not waiting beyond the frontiers; they have already been governing us for quite some time. And it is our consciousness of this that constitutes part of our predicament. We are waiting not for a Godot, but for another – doubtless very different – St Benedict.

(MacIntyre, 1981, pp. 244–5)

Even if MacIntyre's analysis of the contemporary predicament may be questioned, the rediscovery of community and of notions of truth and goodness may once again be a fundamental task before the Church. And in the base communities of Latin America, and in congregations and gatherings of Christians of various types around the world, it is precisely this that is happening.

But in the North there are specific problems in responding to these crises. In the first place, the churches in the North cannot escape the fact that they are predominantly middle class. They are not churches of the poor, and they have great problems in relating to the poor, or demonstrating their relevance to them. This is in some ways even more true of the groups that call themselves house churches and base communities. In Germany, The Netherlands and Britain these are typically gatherings of intellectual middle-class people who are socially concerned and politically committed. When they reach out to the poor they are often greeted with the same kind of suspicion that met the pre-revolutionary Russian idealists, the Narodniks, when they went to the villages to mobilize the peasantry. The mainstream churches at least have a presence among the poor. They are *there*. And sometimes this presence is a channel for communication and learning.

In the second place, there are problems in the relationship between base communities and other informal Christian groups and the institutional Church. In Latin America, as we have seen, the base communities have a tense and critical, but not unconstructive, relationship with the hierarchies. They see an important aspect of their task as challenging the whole Church to *be* the Church. When Leonardo Boff was summoned to Rome and forbidden to write or lecture for a year, he obeyed. Neither he nor the base communities wish to separate themselves from the institutional Church. But in the North 'political prayer meetings' and other groups that see themselves as base communities have an altogether frailer link with the institution. And parishes in poorer areas are sometimes regarded as missions of a powerful and wealthy institution that is solidly middle class in its attitudes and values. Neither situation provides an effective challenge to the institution. The 'base communities' are too loosely connected, and the parishes in poor areas are too dependent upon the human and material resources of the institution. Such units are not in a position to exercise much leverage within the institution.

The third, and most important, problem in seeing the local Christian groups as experiments in community which challenge the power structures of society and provide the basis for a renewal of the Church is parallel to Marx and Engels's criticisms of utopian socialist communities. Marx and Engels saw the numerous contemporary experiments in a socialist and egalitarian lifestyle in little communities as largely distractions from the real issues of power. They did not confront directly structures of injustice and oppression, but provided an escape for a few from the effects of social injustice. Engels regarded the utopian socialist communities initiated by pioneers such as Owen, Fourier and Proudhon as diversions rather than the real engagement. It is possible to criticize many base communities in the North on much the same grounds. Unless they have close links with the institutional Church (which is, after all, part of the power structure of society) and with a popular political movement, they are likely to nourish a romantic idealism and an impotent radicalism.

But we would be wrong to neglect the symbolic value and

force of experiments in fellowship which have an eye to their responsibilities to the broader society, and are capable of combining hope with a realistic assessment of the situation and a keen tactical sense. They have to struggle against the timidity, ingrowth and tendency to be backward-looking which so frequently characterize small groups who dissent from the prevailing values of society. Such communities wait in confidence 'for another – doubtless very different – St Benedict', but they also confront more directly than MacIntyre seems to envisage 'the barbarians' who govern us. They stand both for the rediscovery of fellowship and for the transformation of society. Their waiting upon God and the coming of his Kingdom stirs them to political action, and puts it in its proper perspective.

CHAPTER 7

The Responsibilities of Political Theology

Political theology is contextual theology. It addresses itself to a particular situation at a specific time. This is one reason for the diversity of political theologies; since each is rooted in a particular context, they have rather different agendas and emphases. And, despite its concern with the context, political theology is *theology*, i.e. it endeavours to relate the classical Christian theological tradition to a specific modern situation. Both the classical and the contextual are necessary. The local needs to be related to the universal, the particular to the general, the temporary to the unchanging. Accordingly, we are not concerned with a mass of separate and unconnected contextually specific political theologies, but with a kind of family group, a plurality of theologies with varying emphases, different priorities and varieties of problematic, but sharing a concern to explore the implications in the political realm of the disturbing memory of Jesus Christ.

At the end of chapter 1, it was suggested that there was a kind of spectrum of possible types of political theology, and three positions were explored, defining roughly the extremes and the midpoint of the spectrum. These types of political theology relate to certain general kinds of context, with appropriate modifications in specific cases. A great deal of what followed in this book has been an exploration of Latin American liberation theology, a form of political theology which strongly affirms its own contextuality. This concentration on Latin American material arises because this is the liveliest and most challenging school of political theology today, not because it can be transplanted to a very different context. The Latin Americans themselves deny that their theology can be uprooted and embedded elsewhere. They feel that they themselves have in the past been victims of theological imperialism, made to conform to an alien imported theology which was in fact the theology of the powerful. They eschew any efforts at a kind of counter-imperialism. They tell others to do their own theologizing in relation to their own contexts, learning from the insights of liberation theology and applying them in their own situations. It would be naive and wrong, despite these warnings, to attempt to borrow liberation theology in its entirety, and plant it in an alien soil.

But liberation theology raises a range of issues and questions which challenge and illumine. It offers a method which may work, and must be considered seriously, in other situations. Like other theologies sparked off by a specific crisis, it offers insights and conclusions which have general significance in quite different contexts. And it clarifies and recalls emphases in the classical tradition which have been neglected, obscured or forgotten, for whatever reason. But we must not suppose that liberation theology is the only possibility for a contemporary political theology. In fact there are numerous, very different, political theologies in existence today, as in the past. They have arisen in different contexts and they represent various and conflicting understandings of the function and nature of political theology, and the role of the theologian. And so in this final chapter we return to a critical examination of the spectrum of political theologies outlined in chapter 1, in the expectation that the major types of political theology will be alive and well in the modern world.

CONTEXT AND CRISIS

Four aspects of the context are particularly important for modern political theology: ideology, the economic and political structure of society, the Church and the historical moment. We will consider each in turn.

European political theology, as represented by people such as Moltmann and Metz, tends to devote considerable attention to social processes such as secularization, enlightenment or confining religion to the private sphere and their ideological implications. These are related to general theological themes, such as hope in Bloch and Moltmann. There is little specific and careful economic and class analysis. For example, Moltmann's attempt to set the argument of *The Crucified God* (1974a) in a contemporary frame and show its relevance to the issues of the day seems artificial and unsatisfactory; a very general and somewhat superficial analysis of some of the prominent issues of the late 1960s is tacked rather uneasily onto the substantive theological discussion. There is a tendency to pay more attention to placing political theology in the history of ideas than relating it to its socioeconomic context. Ideology becomes the context for political theology rather than a tool for understanding that context. The conclusion of the Spanish theologian Alfredo Fierro's splendid critical analysis of contemporary political theologies, *The Militant Gospel* (1977), is a case in point. He proposes a theology on the hypothesis of historical materialism. This will take very seriously the determination of ideas and of belief by the economic base, the Marxist convictions about the relation of consciousness to existence and the productive process to social forms. But it will not 'baptize' Marx. This new theology will be critical alike of closed orthodox reductionism and of a self-sufficient and dogmatic Marxist revolutionary movement. It will seek its validation from praxis, and from the future. But the striking point is that Fierro's book, and his concluding constructive proposal in particular, has no reference whatever to the fact that it was written in Spain and no discussion of Spanish, or European, political, social or economic developments. It could have been written almost anywhere. Its explicit materialist statements are contradicted by its assumption that ideas are determinative, and that it is the ideological context that really matters.

By contrast, one cannot read far in liberation theology without coming across social and political analysis, sometimes quite general, but increasingly often specific and intellectually rigorous. There are problems remaining, of course, about how this analysis relates to the theology (in the narrower sense). But it is clear that for the liberation theologians it is the structures of power and class which are the primary elements in the context for political theology. Ideas, while important, are secondary and instrumental. Intellectual debates are not as important as the facts of dominance and dependence, of oppression and struggle which lie behind them. But ideology is an indispensable tool for investigating society, and hence liberation theologians look to social theory, particularly Marxism, for tools with which to investigate society. They have an urgent need for effective means of social analysis; they see Marxism as a system of social analysis which has shown itself appropriate to their conditions, and they believe that they can adopt it as such while paying rather little attention to Marxist metaphysics, or Marxism as a worldview which conflicts at substantial points with Christianity.

The Church provides the third part of the context for political theology. A lively Church, which addresses itself to the major issues on the public agenda and does not become engrossed with its own inner institutional concerns and interests, is likely to produce lively and interesting theology. Where the Church is not involved to a significant extent with the political society in which it is set, and operates as a kind of voluntary organization for people who happen to be interested in religion, its pronouncements are likely to be highly general and rather vacuous. Because it is not itself a functioning part of the political system, it is easy for it to avoid the questions of agency, means and implementation and concern itself entirely with long-term goals and values. It sees its role as moralizing from on high in a way that is not altogether helpful because it takes no account of the ambiguities and limitations of the political realm, and does not commit the Church itself to any action or risk.

Political theology wants to know how the Church understands its social and political role. How is it related to the society, and in particular to the structures of power? What is the class composition of the Church, and how does this affect its public role? But the central question, of course, is how the empirical manifestation of the Church relates to the Kingdom of God, and how far it fulfils its calling to witness to and prefigure that Kingdom.

Most political theology is particularly aware that it has a responsibility for discerning and responding to 'the signs of the times'. It sees itself as responding to a crisis, a *kairos*, a moment of truth. In *The Kairos Document* (1986) to which we will have occasion to refer frequently in this chapter, a group of South African theologians saw themselves as doing precisely this. The crisis of apartheid was the *kairos* for the South African Church:

> A crisis is a judgement that brings out the best in some people and the worst in others. A crisis is a moment of truth that shows us up for what we really are. There will be no place to hide and no way of pretending to be what we are not in fact. At this moment in South Africa the Church is about to be shown up for what it really is and no cover up will be possible.
>
> (Kairos Document, 1986, p. 1)

A crisis is capable of evoking theological insights – but, more important, action: it is 'the moment of grace and opportunity, the favourable time in which God issues a challenge to decisive action' (Kairos Document, 1986, p. 1). And the theology which is evoked, the theology which addresses the present moment, very often has general significance. It is no longer abstract and detached; it tends to be less interested in timeless principles than in the concrete Word of God for the present time. The Bible is not seen legalistically as providing a template for life but as an instrument for discerning the Word of God in the midst of the crisis, a stimulus which alerts us to hear the specific word for today. The crisis of the 1930s of which Nazism was the central phenomenon provoked Dietriech Bonhoeffer both in practice and in his ethics to move from any kind of legalism to a dependence on grace. Karl Barth saw as the central part of his response to the crisis the arduous work of clarifying the content of the Christian faith. He wrote in the first volume of his *Church Dogmatics*, published in German in 1932:

> I believe that as a matter of fact a better church dogmatics (even apart from all utilitarian ethical applications) might be an

ultimately weightier and more solid contribution even to questions and tasks like that of German liberation, than most of the well-meant stuff which so many, even among theologians, think in their dilletantism they should and can supply, with respect to these questions and tasks.

(Barth, 1969 edn, p. xiii)

Such a response is not escaping from the challenge of the *kairos* into abstract theologizing, but contributing at a more profound level so that the response will continue to have significance long after the crisis that evoked it is past.

A theology which strives to to be contextual must understand its context. That means, in the first place, that it looks the facts in the face, that it relates to things as they are rather than some imaginary or unreal world. And this is not a simple thing to do. In Latin America, Paulo Freire developed the process called 'conscientization' in which a basic education in literacy was linked with a heightening of critical awareness of the situation in which people find themselves. It is a process of encouraging people who have been kept in a state of oppression to 'name their world', to confront the facts, to free themselves from the culture of silence and the ideology of oppression. But, as Freire points out, conscientization is more: 'While it involves overcoming false consciousness . . . it implies further the critical insertion of the conscientized person into a demythologized reality . . . There can be no "conscientization" of the people without a radical denunciation of dehumanizing structures, accompanied by the proclamation of a new reality to be created by man' (Freire, 1972–6, pp. 75–6). Conscientization is more than a naive, childish – or childlike – apprehension of the facts; it involves a critical and active grappling with reality understood in the light of a form of social analysis which interprets the situation in terms of oppression and calls for the overthrow of all oppressive structures.

There is here a recognition that there is no such thing as a view of reality which is totally free of ideology, no access to the facts which does not employ some form of social analysis. Because Freire and his fellows see one particular ideology as opening up the facts, and others as forms of false consciousness, the method of conscientization has been denounced by Peter

Berger as an 'elitist exercise in political indoctrination' (quoted in McCann, 1981, p. 2). The choice of an ideology appears to him to be arbitrary and prior to the educative process; it is assumed that 'the facts' are inseparably linked with one particular ideology. But no ideological innocence of the sort Berger appears to be advocating is possible, and Freire uses some Marxist analysis because it appears to be compatible with a Christian orientation and helps people to construe and respond to reality in a Christian way. Futhermore, conscientization is accused of having a built-in reductionism: the 'new reality' is 'to be created by man', and the liberating God of the Bible is identified with the struggle of the oppressed today. Dennis McCann argues that a theology as dependent on conscientization as he believes liberation theology to be ends up taking neither the facts nor the Christian tradition with adequate seriousness because it identifies in an uncritical manner with the struggle of the oppressed (McCann, 1981). It is, however, very doubtful if liberation theology is in fact as dependent on conscientization as McCann suggests, and recent writing by liberation theologians demonstrates both that they take the classical theological tradition with profound seriousness and that they are accordingly not as prone to reductionism as McCann believes.

Professor Raymond Plant has expressed his dismay at the contrast between the substantial and rigorous empirical and normative work done in the social sciences on major social problems and 'the very small amount of independent theological thinking that has been done by the churches on these issues'. He concludes his discussion of Christian social thought in modern Britain by saying, 'until the Church is more intellectually serious about its involvement in politics and tries to link its political and social ethics into a more developed theological understanding of man as a political animal, its claims to be taken seriously in politics will founder' (Plant, 1985, pp. 328–36). One cannot but agree with this assessment, at least as far as Britain is concerned. Elsewhere in the world, there has been a serious and not uncritical engagement with Marxism, both as ideology and as a form of social analysis. What has been particularly lacking is sustained dialogue between theology and other forms of social theory. In contexts where Marxism does not appear particularly convincing there seems to be a profound reluctance to take *any* form of social theory seriously, and a naive assumption that a political theology is possible which is innocent of ideology and of serious social analysis alike. The time is probably past, as William Temple (1881–1944) recognized towards the end of his life, when a 'Christian map of reality' can be constructed. But it is still possible for the theologian to attempt what Reinhold Niebuhr did so successfully – to produce from the Christian theological tradition critical insights about human nature and human society which challenge and enrich thought about social relations and social behaviour.

Any political theology has to work out its relation to current forms of political thought and ideology, learning how to discriminate between them, and how to use them as searchlights to illuminate social reality rather than as blinkers or blindfolds. Above all, it must not accede to the inordinate claims which are so characteristic of political ideologies. Just as there can be no 'pure' theology which does not interact with secular philosophy, so there can be no political theology which simply recounts and responds to the 'brute facts' of social and political life without any interpretation or analysis save that which derives exclusively from the content of the Christian revelation. Political theology must relate to, but dare not become the captive of, the political ideologies of the day if it is to understand the context in which it operates and secure the ability to relate in a Christian and creative way to that situation.

POLITICS AS A VOCATION

In two notable essays, 'Politics as a Vocation' and 'Science as a Vocation', the German sociologist Max Weber distinguished two types of ethics, the ethics of ultimate ends, and the ethics of responsiblity. Religion, he argued, has to do with the ultimate, with moral absolutes, with unconditional obligations; the Sermon on the Mount is a typical instance of a religious ethic. The ethic of responsibility, on the other hand, is a strictly political ethic; it is based on prudence and is not concerned for ultimate horizons but for the dilemmas of imminent decisions. Politics is the realm of compromise, of choices between evils. One cannot survive in politics without accepting and using violence and coercion as necessary tools. Thus Weber argues that the political vocation and religious vocation are totally distinct and in sharp conflict with one another:

> Whoever wants to engage in politics at all, and especially in politics as a vocation, has to realize these ethical paradoxes. I repeat, he lets himself in for the diabolic forces lurking in all violence . . . He who seeks the salvation of the soul, of his own and others, should not seek it along the avenue of politics, for the quite different tasks of politics can only be solved by violence. The genius or demon of politics lives in an inner tension with the God of love, as well as with the Christian God as expressed by the Church. This tension can at any time lead to an irreconcilable conflict.
>
> (Gerth and Mills, 1948, pp. 125–6)

Politics is today, Weber believes, the sphere of realism. Political activity no longer may be orientated by ultimate values in a world which he argues, in deeply pessimistic vein, has been disenchanted. For those who wish to escape from the meaninglessness of acting pragmatically in a disenchanted world, Weber suggests that 'the arms of the Church are opened widely and compassionately' (Gerth and Mills, 1948, p. 155). The fact that Weber speaks in terms of vocation is a reminder of how indebted he was to the Lutheran atmosphere that he breathed from early childhood. Vocation, calling, implies a caller and suggests that somehow behind the sharp conflicts between callings and their associated ethics there is some deeper coherence, because it is the one God who calls different people to particular roles and offices in society. Ultimately, the Lutheran tradition teaches, the varying and often contradictory callings belong together; they form a system, a 'cosmos' of callings'; they complement one another rather than negating one another. Weber also appears to follow Luther in setting the vocation of politics free from direct theological or ethical control: the politician, Luther taught, is responsible directly to God, not to the Church or to the people, for his actions. And Luther agrees with Weber that the politician should act 'realistically', that is, following the rules of prudence or expediency rather than referring constantly to an absolute ethic, even if that be the Sermon on the Mount.

For Weber the sharp disjunction between the political vocation and the religious vocation is not something to be rejoiced in. Politics for him becomes deprived of all ultimate meaning and significance: 'Not summer's bloom lies ahead of us, but rather a polar night of icy darkness and hardness, no matter which group may triumph externally now' (Gerth and Mills, 1948, p. 128). There is no hope to be found in the political world. The profound despair that underlies his analysis of modern secularized society must surely be related to the fact that although he borrows concepts and patterns of thought from Martin Luther, he does not share Luther's faith. He does not believe in even an ultimate reconciliation of the conflicts of this world. There is for him no God who calls people into different vocations and ensures that in their various ways through following out the duties of their callings they are fulfilling the will of God, sometimes despite appearances.

But for political theology the concept of vocation continues to be useful. There is not one, but several, political vocations. The tension between the spiritual calling to faith and all worldly callings, with their associated ethics, is real, but not ultimate, and can be a most creative tension. The realist and the idealist need one another if realism is not to degenerate into a moral and manipulative cynicism and idealism to retain an earthly relevance. Not only do different vocations complement and challenge one another, but particular vocations quite properly come to the fore in specific contexts and times. Different vocations relate to particular ethics, and they generate their own theological emphases as well.

This is so because Christian theology at its heart is not so much a framework or a system of thought, logical, coherent, systematic, as a rational form of response to Jesus Christ. In one sense the theological task is always the same – to proclaim the Gospel – but the mode of fulfilment of this task is very variable. This is partly because theologians no more than anyone else can rise above the relativities, compromises and ambiguities of history and take their stand on the Olympian heights of absolute truth and justice, from where they may judge the deeds of people and nations. They, too, are sinners, they are involved in the relativities of worldly existence, they 'see through a glass darkly', they need to live by forgiveness. They have themselves to strive, and help others as well, to live reasonably and seek peace, justice and freedom in the contexts and vocations in which they find themselves, in quite concrete ways. They have to learn to respond flexibly and lovingly to the demands and questions of their situation, aware always that the possibilities are limited and the best that can be expected still fails far short of the perfect will of God. The task also varies in relation to the audience addressed and the theologian's relation-ship (as pastor, priest or prophet, for instance) to that audience. The theologian is called to 'become all things to everyone', not to please people, or dilute the Gospel, or look after his own interests, but that he 'might by all means save some' (I Cor. 9: 22). The one Gospel is expressed in different and specific ways to different people; it always addresses the whole person in the context of that person's responsibilities, opportunities, vocation and skills, as well as the person's fears and failures and need for forgiveness and encouragement.

We are now in a position to return to the spectrum of possible modes of political theology outlined at the end of chapter 1 and see how these various styles of political theology stand up in the modern world.

EUSEBIAN POLITICAL THEOLOGY

This style of political theology concentrates on the vocation of the ruler. It is the decision-makers who are addressed by theo-logians or churchmen who stand alongside them in the role of chaplain or confessor – or at least it is people in that kind of role who are likeliest to be heard and to have influence. There is a subtle but significant difference between the two terms 'chaplain' and 'confessor'. Both speak from alongside those addressed, with an awareness of the problems they face, but whereas the stress in the term 'chaplain' is on a vague general endorsement of the legitimacy of the activity in which people are engaged, the term 'confessor' suggests a greater awareness that this activity is inherently problematic, that participants require forgiveness for decisions and actions which may be necessary but are not good.

As John Habgood, the Archbishop of York, has argued 'to be close to those in power is to have some first-hand knowledge of the complexity of the actual choices facing them. This has a devastating effect on prophetic certainties. And actually to share responsibility is even more devastating' (Habgood, 1983, p. 105). But decision-makers and the powerful are not the only ones who need sympathy and understanding. Those whose lives are affected by decisions, especially weak and voiceless groups, have an even more pressing right to be heard by the theologian. Sometimes the chaplain or the confessor is in the position of having to relay the voice of the victims to the oppressor. The theologian's task is never to give encouragement to politicians engaged in absurd and immoral policies, but rather to confront evil and proclaim that forgiveness is available for sinners.

The stress in this kind of theology is on responsibility, prudence and wisdom. It must understand the nature and the constraints of responsibility, and the tension between an ethic of responsibility and an ethic of ultimate ends. It is addressed to those who are, or ought to be, aware that their decisions and actions affect the lives and flourishing of many others. They are people whose task is to pursue and advance the legitimate interests of those for whom they are responsible. Part of the theological task in relation to them is to attempt to ensure that these interests are not construed in too narrow or short-term a fashion, and to affirm that responsibility is ultimately to God rather than simply to an electorate. Theology must point steadily towards individual responsibility. Political, economic, scientific and strategic decisions are made and implemented by men and women, and affect men and women. Neither the market with its 'invisible hand' nor the state should be reverenced as powers following their own principles and effectively beyond human control.

The problem with Eusebian theology lies just here. A theology which understands and appreciates the ambiguities and dilemmas faced by the powerful, and sees itself as having a pastoral and supportive role towards them, easily, and usually unconsciously, passes over into the legitimation of the structures of power and collusion with the powerful. It is easy for a court theologian to be corrupted. But a serious political theology cannot refuse to engage with the realities and the limitations of power.

The dangers of a Eusebian theology are highlighted in *The Kairos Document*'s critique of what it calls 'state theology'. This 'is simply the theological justification of the status quo with its racism, capitalism and totalitarianism. It blesses injustice, canonizes the will of the powerful and reduces the poor to passivity, obedience and apathy' (*Kairos Document*, 1986, p. 3). It twists Scripture to serves its purposes. It declares its own understanding of law and order to be divinely sanctioned, denounces those who challenge it as ungodly, and demands for the state an obedience which should be reserved for God alone. It proclaims that communism is the ultimate evil, and sets up a god of the state who is in fact an idol, 'a god who exalts the proud and humbles the poor'. The god of the South African state is blasphemously invoked in the preamble to the apartheid constitution: 'in humble submission to almighty God, who controls the destinies of nations and the histories of peoples; who gathered our forebears together from many lands and gave them this their own; who has guided them from generation to generation; who has wondrously delivered them from dangers that beset them (*Kairos Document*, 1986, p. 6). This, the *Kairos* theologians say, 'is not merely an idol or false god, it is the devil disguised as Almighty God – the antichrist' (*Kairos Document*, 1986, p. 8). State theology is heretical and blasphemous.

The state theology of South Africa is, of course, an extreme case. But there have been even worse instances in modern times – the 'German Christian' support for Hitler and his attempted extermination of the Jewish people is a case in point. Such instances are important as warnings of what can happen, of how easily this style of political theology can tip over into complicity in oppression and injustice. But political theology must not shirk addressing the powerful and attending to the dilemmas and problems that they face. A necessary awareness that the corridors of power are dangerous places does not justify the theologian in deserting them to cultivate in detachment a supposedly 'pure' and apolitical theology. Like any other system of ideas, theology can easily be sucked into becoming little more than an ideology justifying the ways of the powerful to themselves and to those without power, Christian on the surface, but in substance and effect pure 'civil theology' with a thin coating of Christian rhetoric. The theologian should be close to the powerful and the experts, but not 'at home' among them – familiar with the corridors of power, but not at ease within them. For theology is both a speaking of truth to power and a voice for the powerless and marginalized, for the victims, who have a special place in the Kingdom. Such a theology, addressed constructively to the decision-makers, in such a way that the weak and the powerless and the excluded may overhear, is the most honest and the most authentic support than can be given them in their complex task and responsibility.

CHURCH POLITICAL THEOLOGY

This is the approach to political theology which we associated with the name of Tertullian. The theologian addresses the state and civil society from within the Church, which is seen as a kind of alternative community, a model that society might emulate and an earnest of God's purposes for all humankind. The theologian does not enter the discussion as a free-floating expert, a specialist in speculation about divine things, but as a mouthpiece for the household of faith, someone who represents a particular tradition and community of faith. This is not to deny that the theologian's attitude to the tradition may often be critical, and the relationship with the Church an uneasy one. But the theologian represents a catholic, worldwide fellowship which is the contemporary manifestation of the tradition and which shares the responsibility for the doing of theology. Theology is a function of the whole Church; the theologian does not have a monopoly of theologizing and should be attentive, but not submissive, to the thinking of the whole Church. Theologians and Church leaders today have to remember that their statements and interventions are being monitored by churches and Christians throughout the world. They should welcome the opportunity to test their views and their assessments against those of other Christians.

There are, of course, dangers in Church theology. The theologian may be effectively trapped within a Church which understands itself primarily as a state or national church and cannot put issues in a broader frame than that of the national interest. The theologian may see the task as defending the institutional interests and promulgating the official views of the institutional Church. This kind of theology becomes diplomatic, the very antithesis of prophecy. Church theology often slips into a naive conviction that the Church is an unambiguous sign of the Kingdom, that the Church is above criticism; this kind of naivety leads quickly to triumphalism and ecclesiastical arrogance, on the one hand, and a refusal to do or say anything that might put the prosperity or standing of the Church at risk, on the other.

Once again *The Kairos Document* spotlights the dangers attendant upon Church political theology. This kind of theology is depicted as critical of apartheid in a limited, guarded and cautious way. 'Its criticism,' the authors continue, 'is superficial and counterproductive, because instead of engaging in an in depth analysis of the signs of the times, it relies upon a few stock ideas derived from Christian tradition and then uncritically and repeatedly applies them to our situation' (*Kairos Document*, 1986, p. 9). The main concepts are reconciliation, justice and non-violence. The reconciliation or peace of which they speak is a false and easy peace, disjoined from justice. This is reconciliation without repentance, peace without facing the issues of justice and oppression which make for conflict, a false peace and a counterfeit reconciliation. It is a theology of reconciliation with sin and the devil, rather than 'a biblical theology of direct confrontation with the forces of evil'.

Church theology seeks a justice of reform through appeals to the government or to the white minority. But the writers argue, 'God does not bring his justice through reforms introduced by the Pharaohs of this world' (*Kairos Document*, 1986, p. 12). While appeals to the conscience of the powerful must be made, individual conversion is not enough; it is necessary to attend to 'the more radical justice that comes from below and is determined by the people of South Africa'. Church pronouncements tend to condemn 'all violence', but in practice to be far more stringent on the responsive, despairing violence of the oppressed than on the systematic and ruthless violence of the state apparatus. More and more people are asking on whose side the Church theologians stand, for they seem implicitly to accept the legitimacy of the regime and to strive to maintain a form of neutrality which 'enables the status quo of oppression (and therefore violence) to continue. It is a way of giving tacit support to the oppressor, a support for brutal violence' (*Kairos Document*, 1986, p. 15). Church theology does not understand the mechanisms of injustice and oppression because it has not been able to develop an adequate form of social analysis. It has little understanding of politics and political strategy, and makes a virtue out of sitting on the fence. All this rests on a fundamentally inadequate understanding of the faith and of spirituality, as having little to do with the life of the world, and regarding passivity as a virtue. It is this unbiblical approach which 'leaves so many Christians and Church leaders in a state of near paralysis' in face of the present crisis in South Africa.

This may be a fair criticism in the context of South Africa today, but there is a need for an authentic Church political theology. A theology which does not take the Church seriously is fundamentally defective. If Church leaders are reluctant to put the unity of the Church under strain and hesitate to issue divisive prophetic statements, it is because they see the importance of maintaining the Church as some kind of demonstration that reconciliation is possible, because they correctly conclude that prophets need a base, and the Church is capable of providing just such a supportive context for more outspoken groups or individuals, and because they believe that the Church is necessary for the sustaining of vision, of a sense of direction, of ultimate values. But, taken to extremes, this approach can lead to collusion with evil.

Vision, values, goals are what Péguy meant by 'mystique'. He suggested that mystique provided (*a*) a shared vision, the common goals, the underlying degree of value consensus which is necessary for healthy community life; (*b*) a powerful source of motivation for relatively disinterested and imaginative work in the civil community; (*c*) an effective sustaining force for those who bear the burden of taking difficult decisions which affect the destiny of others (Péguy, 1958).

First, a mystique provides a vision of reality, a horizon within which life is lived and decisions are taken. John Habgood puts the point well:

> The prime Christian contribution to social ethics is in the indicative rather than the imperative mood. In terms of the principles by which people should live and societies order themselves, Christians have little to say that could not be said by any reasonable person of good will. It is Christian belief about the kind of place the world is, about the depth of human sinfulness and the possibilities of divine grace, about judgement and hope, incarnation and salvation, God's concern for all and his care for each, about human freedom and divine purpose – it is beliefs such as these which make the difference, and provide the context within which the intractible realities of social and political life can be tackled with wisdom and integrity.
>
> (Habgood, 1983, p. 168)

But more needs to be said. The vision is not only in the indicative mood; it includes principles, imperatives and narrative as well as abstract statements. It is more than a neutral backdrop to the drama of politics; it is a disturbing challenge to the action and its ends. The principles within the vision may often appear to be fairly general, uncontroversial and imprecise. Their bearing upon specific policy options and particular decisions is often so vague that we might be tempted to agree with Enoch Powell that there are no logical bridges across the gulf between the assertions of Christianity and the conduct of the world's business (Powell, 1977, p. 30–51). But then, lest we conclude too hastily that the vision gives no guidance in things that really matter, we find that it generates quite specific imperatives in relation to Nazism, or apartheid, to name but two areas where there is a fairly broad Christian consensus. This suggests that there is a movement from vision to policy, from the indicative to the imperative, which is authentic, if not always as clear as in the two cases just instanced. It always remains fairly general, so that it tells us that apartheid must be opposed but it does not indicate how, or what system should take its place. R. H. Tawney is right that one cannot explain a principle without reference to the policies through which it could be put into practice. But because policies are so much more contentious than principles, Church spokesmen repeatedly lay down general principles which have little specific content and few clear policy implications.

But the mystique does not generate a systematic Christian political ideology. It is not a grand theory, but a fascinating set of fragments. These provide a view of reality which should enable people to cut through mystifications and distortions, whether generated by political ideologies or otherwise, in order to see things as they really are and respond to them in a proper, that is a loving and honest, way. Just as the little boy in Hans Christian Anderson's story was the only one to trust the evidence of his senses, the only one who was not manipulated into denying the truth, and cried out, 'But the Emperor has no clothes on!', so the Christian in childlikeness should contribute to the political process a reverence for truth and a trusting openness to people. Beyond that, what the mystique does is to provide an increased awareness of the heights and depths of which human beings are capable – and the recognition that even 'reasonable people of good will' have a great capacity for self-delusion, and for unconsciously twisting things to serve their interests.

In the second place, the mystique provides motivation. There are, of course, many sources of motivation, and motives are always mixed. Pure altruism is a rare commodity. The mystique encourages a curbing or setting aside of selffishness in order to seek a higher good. And, more important still, it nourishes a pertinacity and steadfastness in the face of adversity and unpopularity which is a major asset in democratic politics as long as it does not degenerate into stubbornness.

Thirdly, the mystique nourishes politics by sustaining those who have to cope with the tensions, ambiguities and problems of policy-making and the taking of decisions. It offers not just guidance and challenge, but forgiveness, for in this fallen, broken world there is no such thing as purity or innocence in politics; we must act and we must decide as responsibly as may be, relying on God's grace to make up our deficiencies and give us the courage to continue.

Without a Church which is still capable of attending to people's condition, which stands, however haltingly, for justice, human dignity and decency, and cares about the poor and the powerless, no Christian political theology is possible – so much would be admitted even by the authors of *The Kairos Document*. They challenge the Church to *be* the Church, to be the steward of the mystique rather than the nervous defender of its own institutional interests.

PROPHETIC THEOLOGY

The midpoint in the spectrum of possible types of political theology was related in our original formulation to the thought of Augustine. A search for modern equivalents of the Augustinian political theology reveals a number of possibilities. The thought of Reinhold Niebuhr, and the school of Christian realism derived from him, is clearly much indebted to Augustine's thought. In another way liberation theology stands in the Augustinian tradition. And it could be suggested that what *The Kairos Document* calls 'prophetic theology' is quite close in a number of ways to the Augustinian approach. None of these provides a perfect fit, as it were, but they should be placed in the same sector of the spectrum, for all are aware of the dangers facing a 'court theology' and the limitations of a purely ecclesiastical theology. They seek to relate today's society to the life of the Kingdom and are sensitive both to the ambiguities and constraints of the political system and to the challenging and already partially realized hope of the Kingdom of justice and of peace.

The writers of *The Kairos Document* call for a response to the present crisis which is biblical, spiritual, pastoral and, above all, prophetic. This involves, they believe, turning to the Bible to find hints and clues which will be helpful in reading the signs of the times. Prophetic theology is not systematic or academic; it tends to be disjointed and fragmentary; but it, unlike academic theology, is always a call to action, a summons to repentance, conversion and change. It is a proclamation of the Gospel:

> It will *denounce* sin and *announce* salvation. But to be prophetic our theology must name the sins and the evils that surround us and the salvation that we are hoping for. Prophecy must name the sins of apartheid, injustice, oppression and tyranny in South Africa today as 'an offence against God' and the measures which must be taken to overcome these sins and the suffering that they cause. On the other hand prophecy will announce the hopeful good news of future liberation, justice and peace, as God's will and promise, naming the ways of bringing this about and encouraging people to take action.
>
> (*Kairos Document*, 1986, p. 18)

Prophetic theology also demands social analysis. When this is put together with insights from the Bible, it becomes necessary first to tell the truth, to declare the emperor's nakedness, to denounce the apartheid regime as 'A tyrant. A totalitarian regime. A reign of terror'. It is irreformable. But just as the Bible does not simply describe oppression, sin and injustice as offences against God, but announces that God will liberate and forgive, so it is necessary to say that apartheid must be, and will be, removed. For the prophetic word is at its heart a message of hope, and hope for all but especially for the oppressed. And prophetic theology is always and everywhere a challenge to action – in the case of contemporary South Africa taking sides with the oppressed, participating in the struggle for liberation, refusing to collaborate with tyranny, and praying, thinking and working for a change in government.

This highlights characteristics and problems involved in prophetic theology. It understands itself as a confessional matter, simultaneously the proclamation of the Gospel and of the implications of the Gospel. Indeed, it is often suggested that it is radically distorting to separate the two. It is impossible to proclaim the Gospel without also denouncing false gospels. Thus, in 1934, the representatives of the Confessing Church in Germany, led by Karl Barth and Martin Niemoller, in the Theological Declaration of Barmen, affirmed the truth of the Gospel and declared Nazism to be incompatible with this Gospel. And the Joint Theological Commission of the South African Council of Churches and the South African Catholic Bishops' Conference produced *A Message to the People of South Africa* where, after a credal affirmation, they went on to declare that apartheid is:

> a false faith, a novel Gospel which offers happiness and peace for the community and for the individual. It holds out to men a security built not upon Christ but on the theory of separation and the preservation of their racial identity. It presents separate development of our race groups as a way for the people of South Africa to save themselves. Such a claim inevitably conflicts with the Christian gospel, which offers salvation, both social and individual, through faith in Christ alone.
>
> (Gruchy and Villa-Vicencio, 1983, p. 155)

Underlying this approach to political theology is the belief that within the complexities of the situation there is a simple, yet hard and costly, choice: in whom do we put our trust? Is the Gospel true, or is truth to be found elsewhere? Yet choices are not always as clearcut as in the two situations we have mentioned. There are dangers in refusing to recognize the ambiguities and complexities of a situation, and equally in failing to attend to the underlying, and often simple, issues at stake. It is perhaps not often that the Church can take a confessional stance, moving directly from credal statement and social analysis to a political affirmation. But sometimes this is what the Church must do, as Dietrich Bonhoeffer realized: 'The church must be able to say the Word of God, the word of authority, here and now, in the most concrete way possible, from knowledge of the situation. The church may not therefore preach timeless principles, however true, but only commandments which are true today. God is "always" *God* to us "*today*" ' (Bonhoeffer, 1965, p. 161f).

Max Horkheimer of the Franfurt School has written: 'Behind every genuinely human action stands theology . . . a politics which . . . does not preserve a theological movement in itself is, no matter how skillful, in the last analysis, mere business' (in Davis, 1980, p. 18). Without this 'theological moment' politics is reduced to horse-trading, compromises, trade-offs, jockeying for power with no ultimate end in view – petty politics without any exalted aim: purely and simply a battle of individual and collective interests, with the prize to the strongest. Faithfulness demands of Christian theology that it remain in the public realm and engages in depth with the complexities of political life. For the issues of politics are intimately related to the proclamation of the Kingdom, which has to do with liberation in the profoundest and most comprehensive sense. Theology's proper service is to help people to see the problems and conflicts of the day *sub specie aeternitatis*, in the broad frame of God's purposes of love and justice, and his special care for the poor and the oppressed.

References

Anderson, Gerald H. and Stransky, T. F., (eds) (1979) *Mission Trends 4 - Liberation Theologies*. New York: Paulist Press; Grand Rapids: Eerdmans.

Apostolic Fathers (1867) *The Writings of the Apostolic Fathers*. Ante-Nicene Christian Libray, series eds, James Donaldson and Alexander Roberts. Edinburgh: T. and T. Clark.

Archbishop of Canterbury's Commission on Urban Priority Areas (1985) *Faith in the City*. London: Church House Publishing.

Augustine (1945) *The City of God*, 2 vols. London: Dent.

Barth, Karl (1939) *Church and State*. London: SCM Press.

Barth, Karl (1954) *Against the Stream*. London: SCM Press.

Barth, Karl (1969) *Church Dogmatics*, I/1. Edinburgh: T. and T. Clark.

Becker, Carl (1932) *The Heavenly City of the Eighteenth Century Philosophers*. New Haven: Yale University Press.

Belo, Fernando (1981) *A Materialist Reading of the Gospel of Mark*. Maryknoll: Orbis.

Bentley, James (1982) *Between Christ and Marx: The Dialogue in German-Speaking Europe, 1870–1970*. London: Verso.

Bloch, Ernst (1918) *Geist Der Utopie*. Munich and Leipzig: von Duncker und Humblot.

Bloch, Ernst (1972) *Atheism in Christianity*. New York: Herder and Herder.

Bloch, Ernst (1986) *The Principle of Hope*, 3 vols. Oxford: Basil Blackwell.

Boff, Leonardo (1980) *Jesus Christ Liberator: a Critical Christology of Our Time*. London: SPCK.

Boff, Leonardo (1985) *Church: Charism and Power*. London: SCM Press.

Bonhoeffer, Dietrich (1956) *Letters and Papers from Prison*. London: SCM Press.

Bonhoeffer, Dietrich (1965) *No Rusty Swords: Letters, Lectures and Notes 1928-1936*. London: Collins.

Bonino, José Miguez (1975) *Revolutionary Theology Comes of Age*. London: SPCK.

Bonino, José Miguez (ed.) (1984) *Faces of Jesus: Latin American Christologies*. Maryknoll: Orbis.

Brown, Peter (1967) *Augustine of Hippo – A Biography*. London: Faber.

Calvin, John (1961) *Institutes of the Christian Religion*, edited by John T. McNeill; translated by F. L. Battles. London: SCM Press.

Calvin, John (1875) *Letter to the King of England*. In *Corpus Reformatorum*, XIV, 40. Brunswick: Schwetschke.

Cardenal, Ernesto (1977-82) *The Gospel in Solentiname*, 4 vols. Maryknoll: Orbis.

Catherwood, H. F. R. (1964) *The Christian in Industrial Society*. London: IVP.

Catherwood, H.F.R. (1975) *A Better Way: The Case for a Christian Social Order*. London: IVP.

Catherwood, H. F. R. (1979) *First Things First*. Tring: Lion.

Chenu, M. D. (1977) Vatican II and the church of the poor. *Concilium*, 104.

Clévenot Michel (1985) *Materialist Approaches to the Bible*. Maryknoll: Orbis.

Comblin, Joseph (1985) Monotheism and popular religion. *Concilium*, 177.

Commission on Theological Concerns of the Christian Conference of Asia (1983) *Minjung Theology: People as the Subjects of History*. Maryknoll: Orbis.

Coulanges, Fustel de (1956) *The Ancient City*. New York: Doubleday Anchor.

Cox, Harvey (1965) *The Secular City*. London: SCM Press.

Cox, Harvey (1984) *Religion in the Secular City*. New York: Simon and Schuster.

Croatto, Severino (1982) Biblical hermeneutics in the theology of the oppressed. *Vidyajyoti*, February.

Cullmann, Oscar (1951) *Christ and Time*. London: SCM Press.

Cullmann, Oscar (1957) *The State in the New Testament*. London: SCM Press.

Davis, Charles (1980) *Theology and Political Society*. Cambridge: Cambridge University Press.

Douglas, Mary (1970) *Natural Symbols*. Harmondsworth: Penguin.

Dumas, André (1978) *Political Theology and the Life of the Church.* London: SCM Press,

Dunstan, Gordon (1982) Theological method in the deterrence debate. In: G. Goodwin (ed.) *Ethics and Nuclear Deterrence.* London: Croom Helm.

Ehrhardt, Arnold A. T. (1959–1969) *Politische Metaphysik von Solon bis Augustin,* 3 vols. Tübingen: J. C. B. Mohr.

Eliot, T. S. (1939) *The Idea of a Christian Society.* London: Faber and Faber.

Fierro, Alfredo (1977) *The Militant Gospel – An Analysis of Contemporary Political Theologies.* London: SCM Press.

Forrester, Duncan B. (1980) *Caste and Christianity.* London: Curzon Press.

Frankfort, Henri et al. (1949) *Before Philosophy – the Intellectual Adventure of Ancient Man.* Harmondsworth: Penguin.

Freire, Paulo (1972a) *Pedagogy of the Oppressed.* Harmondsworth: Penguin.

Freire, Paulo (1972b) *Cultural Action for Freedom.* Harmondsworth: Penguin.

Garaudy, Roger (1976) *The Alternative Future: A Vision of Christian Marxism.* Harmondsworth: Penguin

Gardavsky, Vitezslav (1973) *God Is Not Yet Dead.* Harmondsworth: Penguin.

Gerassi, John (ed.) (1973) *Camilo Torres: Revolutionary Priest.* Harmondsworth: Penguin.

Gerth, H. H. and Mills, C. Wright (1948) *From Max Weber: Essays in Sociology.* London: Routledge and Kegan Paul.

Gheerbrant, Alain (1974) *The Rebel Church in Latin America.* Harmondsworth: Penguin.

Gibellini, Rosino (ed.) (1980) *Frontiers of Theology in Latin America.* London: SCM Press.

Glatzer, Nahum N. (ed.) (1969) *The Passover Haggada.* New York: Schocken Books.

Gottwald, Norman (1979) *The Tribes of Jahweh: A Sociology of the Religion of Liberated Israel, 1250–1050 BCE.* Maryknoll: Orbis.

Gottwald, Norman (ed.) (1983) *The Bible and Liberation: Political and Social Hermeneutics.* Maryknoll: Orbis.

Gruchy, John de and Villa-Vicencio, Charles (eds) (1983) *Apartheid Is a Heresy.* Guildford: Lutterworth Press.

Gutierrez, Gustavo (1974) *A Theology of Liberation.* London: SCM Press.

Gutierrez, Gustavo (1977) The poor in the church. *Conilium,* 104.

Gutierrez, Gustavo (1983) *The Power of the Poor in History*. London: SCM Press.

Habermas, Jürgen (1976) *Legitimation Crisis*. London: Heinemann.

Habermas, Jürgen (1981) *Theorie des kommunikativen Handelns*, 2 vols. Frankfurt: Suhrkamp.

Habgood, John (1983) *Church and Nation in a Secular Age*. London: Darton, Longman and Todd.

Hanke, Lewis (1959) *Aristotle and the American Indians*. London: Hollis and Carter.

Herberg, William (1960) *Protestant, Catholic, Jew*. New York: Doubleday.

Johnson, Paul (1976) *A History of Christanity*. Harmondsworth: Penguin.

Jowett, Benjamin (1945) *The Four Socratic Dialogues of Plato*. Oxford: Clarendon Press.

Kairos Document (1986) London: British Council of Churches.

Kant, Emmanuel (1949) *The Philosophy of Kant*. New York: The Modern Library.

Kautsky, Karl (1953 edn) *Foundations of Christianity*. New York: Russell and Russell.

Kee, Alastair (1974) *A Reader in Political Theology*. London: SCM Press.

Kee, Alastair (1982) *Constantine or Christ?* London: SCM Press.

Kuitert, H. M. (1986) *Everything is Politics but Politics is not Everything – A Theological Perspective on Faith and Politics*. London: SCM Press.

Küng, Hans (1968) *The Church*. London: Search Press.

Lane, Christel (1981) *The Rites of Rulers: Ritual in Industrial Society – The Soviet Case*. Cambridge: Cambridge University Press.

van Leeuwen, Arendt Th. (1964) *Christianity in World History*. London: Edinburgh House.

Lowrie, Walter (1962) *Kierkegaard*. New York: Harper Torchbooks.

Luther, Martin (1955–) *American Edition of Luther's Works*, edited by Jaroslav Pelikan and H. T. Lehman, St Louis: Concordia and Philadelphia: Muhlenberg Press (AE).

Luther, Martin (1915-32) *Philadelphia Edition of Martin Luther's Works*. Philadelpia: A. J. Holman Company (PE).

McCann, Dennis P. (ed.) (1981): *Christian Realism and Liberation Theology: Practical Theologies in Creative Conflict*. Maryknoll: Orbis.

Machiavelli, Niccolo (1950) *The Prince and The Discourses*. New York: The Modern Library.

Machovec, Milan (1976) *A Marxist Looks at Jesus*. London: Darton, Longman and Todd.

MacIntyre, Alastair (1981) *After Virtue: a Study in Moral Theory*. London: Duckworth.

McLellan, David (1977) *Karl Marx: Selected Writings*. Oxford: Basil Blackwell.

Martin, David (1980) *The Breaking of the Image: A Sociology of Christian Theory and Practice*. Oxford: Basil Blackwell.

Martin, David (1981) *No Alternative: The Prayer Book Controversy*. Oxford: Basil Blackwell.

Marx, Karl and Engels, Frederick (1957) *On Religion*. Moscow: Foreign Languages Publishing House.

Metz, Johann Baptist (1980) *Fatih in History and Society*. London: Burns and Oates.

Miranda, José P. (1977) *Marx and the Bible: A Critique of the Philosophy of Oppression*. London: SCM Press.

Mojzes, Paul (ed.) (1978) *Varieties of Christian Marxist Dialogue*. Philadelphia: The Ecumenical Press.

Moltmann, Jürgen (1967) *Theology of Hope*. London: SCM Press.

Moltmann, Jürgen (1974a) *The Crucified God*. London: SCM Press.

Moltmann, Jürgen (1974b) *Religion and Political Society*. New York: Harper and Row.

Moltmann, Jürgen (1975) *The Experiment Hope* London: SCM Press.

Moltmann, Jürgen (1978) *The Church in the Power of the Spirit*. London: SCM Press.

Moltmann, Jürgen (1981) *The Trinity and the Kingdom of God*. London: SCM Press.

Morrison, Clinton D. (1960) *The Powers That Be*. London: SCM Press.

Munby, Denys (1963) *The Idea of a Secular Society and its Significance for Christians*. London: Oxford University Press.

Newbigin, Lesslie (1983) *The Other Side of 1984*. London: British Council of Churches.

Nineham, Dennis (1976) *The Use and Abuse of the Bible*. London: Macmillan.

Norman, Edward R. (1979) *Christianity and the World Order*. London: Oxford University Press.

Ogletree, Thomas W. (1984) *The Use of the Bible in Christian Ethics*. Oxford: Basil Blackwell.

Péguy, Charles (1958) *Temporal and Eternal*. London: Harvill Press.

Peterson, Erik (1935) *Der Monotheismus als politisches Problem*. In: *Theologische Tractate* (1951). Munich: Kösel-Verlag.

Pixley, George V. (1981) *God's Kingdom*. London: SCM Press.

Plant, Raymond (1985) The Anglican Church and the secular state. In:

George Moyser (ed.) *Church and Politics Today*. Edinburgh: T. and T. Clark.

Powell, Enoch (1977) *Wrestling with the Angel*. London: Sheldon Press.

Preston, Ronald (1981) *Explorations in Theology 9*. London: SCM Press.

Richard, Pablo (1984) The church of the poor within the popular movement, *Concilium*, 176.

Richardson, Alan (1952) *The Biblical Doctrine of Work*. London: SCM Press.

Riesman, David (1951) *The Lonely Crowd*. New Haven: Yale University Press.

Rousseau, J. J. (1947) *Social Contract*. London: Oxford University Press.

Rowland, Christopher (1985) *Christian Origins*. London: SPCK.

Ruggieri, Giuseppe (1985) God and power – a political function of monotheism? *Concilium*, 177, pp. 16–27.

Sanders, E. P. (1985) *Jesus and Judaism*. London: SCM Press.

Sanders, Jack T. (1976) *Ethics in the New Testament*. London: SCM Press.

Schottroff, Willy and Stegemann, Wolfgang (eds) (1984) *God of the Lowly: Socio-historical Interpretations of the Bible*. Maryknoll: Orbis.

Schrey, Heinz-Horst, Walz, Hans Hermann and Whitehouse, W. A. (1955) *The Biblical Doctrine of Justice and Law*. London: SCM Press.

Schweitzer, Albert (1910) *The Quest of the Historical Jesus*. London: A. and C. Black.

Scruton, Roger (1980) *The Meaning of Conservatism*. Harmondsworth: Penguin.

Segundo, Juan Luis (1977) *The Liberation of Theology*. Dublin: Gill and Macmillan.

Segundo, Juan Luis (1985) *The Historical Jesus of the Synoptics*. Maryknoll: Orbis.

Shiner, Larry (1966) *The Secularization of History. An Introduction to the Theology of Friedrich Gogarten*. Nashville: Abingdon.

Sobrino, Jon (1978) *Christology at the Crossroads*. London: SCM Press.

Sobrino, Jon (1985) *The True Church and the Poor*. London: SCM Press.

Sölle, Dorothee (1974) *Political Theology*. Philadelphia: Fortress.

Sophocles (1947) *Theban Plays*, translated by E. F. Watling. Harmondsworth: Penguin.

Tawney, R. H. (1926) *Religion and the Rise of Capitalism*. London: Allen and Unwin.

Tertullian (1869–70) *The Writings of Tertullian*. Ante-Nicene Christian Library, 3 vols, series eds, James Donaldson and Alexander Roberts. Edinburgh: T. and T. Clark.

Torrance, David (ed.) (1982) *The Witness of the Jews to God*. Edinburgh: Handsel.

Torres, Sergio and Eagleson, John (eds) (1981) *The Challenge of Basic Christian Communities*. Maryknoll: Orbis.

Turner, Bryan S. (1983) *Religion and Social Theory*. London: Heinemann.

Williams, George H. (1951) Christology and church–state relations in the fourth century. *Church History*, 20. pp. 4, 5.

Willmer, Haddon (ed.) (1979) *Christianity and Political Hopes*. London: Epworth.

Wink, Walter (1975) *The Bible and Human Transformation*. Philadelphia: Fortress.

Wink, Walter (1984) *Naming the Powers: the Language of Power in the New Testament*. Philadelphia: Fortress Press.

Witvliet, Theo (1985) *A Place in the Sun*. London: SCM Press.

Wolin, Sheldon (1961) *Politics and Vision: Continuity and Innovation in Western Political Thought*. London: Allen and Unwin.

Wright, G. Ernest (1954) *The Biblical Doctrine of Man in Society*. London: SCM Press.

Young, Frances (1983) *From Nicaea to Chalcedon*, London: SCM Press.

Index